WEAVER
on
Strategy

Also by EARL WEAVER

It's What You Learn After You Know It All That Counts
with Berry Stainback

Winning!
edited by John Sammis

WEAVER on Strategy

The Classic Work on the Art of
Managing a Baseball Team

EARL WEAVER with Terry Pluto

Potomac Books
An imprint of the University of Nebraska Press

Library of Congress Cataloging-in-Publication Data

Weaver, Earl, 1930–
    Weaver on strategy : the classic work on the art of managing a baseball team / Earl Weaver with Terry Pluto.—Rev. 2002 ed.
      p. cm.
    ISBN 1-57488-424-7 (pbk.) — 978-1-61234-514-7 (electronic edition)
    1. Weaver, Earl, 1930—   2. Baseball—Management.   3. Baseball managers—United States—Biography. I. Pluto, Terry, 1955– II. Title.
GV875.7 .W43   2002
796.357'06'9—dc21   2002066687

CONTENTS

INTRODUCTION

Earl Weaver spent twenty-eight years managing baseball teams. In twenty-one of those years his club finished in first or second place. Only twice, in his first full year as a minor-league skipper, and in his last year in the majors, did Weaver manage a team that lost more games than it won.

They can talk about Weaver's spats with the umpires, his occasional verbal volleys with his players, or his candid personality, but in the end the one thing that raised Weaver above the rest of the game's managers was that he won. He did it year after year. Weaver won with young teams and veteran teams, teams that hit home runs and teams that stole bases. He won in Elmira, Rochester, Baltimore—even Fox Cities. He won when the experts said he should, and he won when they said he wouldn't. No other manager can claim such a gaudy record over a quarter of a century. Among big-league managers, only Joe McCarthy has a higher winning percentage than Weaver.

"I think Earl Weaver would have been a success no matter what he did for a living," says Harry Dalton, general manager of the Milwaukee Brewers. "He has a quick mind. His organizational abilities and his knack for understanding statistics are outstanding. He is not afraid to make a decision and stick with it. He has plenty of guts and can get the most out of any baseball team."

To understand how Weaver won, you have to know something about the kind of person Earl Weaver is. It all began for Earl in St. Louis. His father ran a dry cleaning firm, and among his clients were the St. Louis Cardinals and the St. Louis Browns. The Weaver family made many trips to Sportsman's Park.

"As a kid, I would carry the uniforms in and out of the clubhouse," says Weaver. "In my mind, there never was a doubt that I'd make the majors. Between the Cards and the Browns, I would go to a hundred games a year. I had a 'Me and Paul' T-shirt. I loved the old Gas House Gang with Pepper Martin, Joe Medwick, Dizzy and Paul Dean.''

The 1934 St. Louis Cardinals played hard. Well, maybe more than just hard. They didn't just break up double plays, they knocked the pivoting second baseman flat. They talked big and won big. They were a team that really did try to run through walls in order to beat the opposition.

Earl watched that team and the St. Louis clubs that followed. By the age of thirteen he was constantly in the grandstand, second-guessing Cardinals' manager Billy Southworth—and Southworth was a fine manager, with a .593 winning percentage.

At five feet six inches and 145 pounds, Earl lacked the classic big-league build. In the summer he played for his father. As Earl Weaver, Sr., loved to recall, his team won four straight summer-league pennants with his son at second base. Earl also had an outstanding career at Beaumont High, and after his senior year the Browns and the Cardinals were both after him. He chose the Cards when minor-league director Walter Shannon pointed toward second base at Sportsman's Park and told Earl, ''One day you'll play there.''

That was exactly what seventeen-year-old Earl Weaver thought. So he signed a contract and went to the Cardinals' minor-league complex in Albany, Georgia. When he arrived, they gave him a uniform with No. 521 on the back. It was then that he fully realized how far away he was from second base at Sportsman's Park.

He was one of ten second basemen taking ground balls during those early workouts. ''You had the feeling that if you missed one, you were gone,'' he remembers. ''They were cutting guys left and right.''

So he didn't miss. He made it through spring training—a notable feat in itself—and began his pro career at West Frankfort, Illinois.

Like thousands of minor leaguers across the country, Earl rode the buses. He grew tough on the $1.25-a-day meal money. He learned to play when the temperature was 32 degrees and when it was 102 degrees. In his second year of pro ball, he drove in 101 runs while hitting only two homers. In two of his first four years,

Earl was named Most Valuable Player in his league. Perhaps more significantly, all four of his teams won titles.

But after eight years of beating the bushes, Weaver realized he would never make the majors. So late in the 1956 season, he became the player-manager of the Knoxville Smokies. The following year he was hired to run the Orioles' Class D club in Fitzgerald, Georgia. As a player, Weaver had started at the bottom. He was doing the same as a manager, only this time he made it to the top.

"If some people are natural players, then I believe Earl Weaver was a natural manager," says former Baltimore Orioles' minor-league director Jim McLaughlin, who gave Weaver that first job at Fitzgerald. "He is a great judge of talent. He knew how to handle players. Those are gifts like having a strong arm or good speed."

"When I started managing in the minors, I never thought about getting to the big leagues," Earl insists. "Of course, that's what everyone in the minors wants. But I didn't think it would happen to me. I was happy to have a job in baseball, and I did it as well as I could."

Earl Weaver always did very well both on and off the field. Perhaps there is a connection.

"I had a lot of different jobs in the winter," says Weaver. "I believe I've run into about every kind of person you can imagine. I know how to get along in any type of setting. This may have helped me in baseball because the people are so varied.

"They loved me at Liberty Loan," comments Weaver. "I took a test before I got the job and achieved the highest score they ever had. I don't believe I ever made a bad loan for them. I've heard all the excuses about the check being in the mail and so on. I could look into a person's eyes and tell if he would be a good candidate for a loan."

He also was an effective used-car salesman. That was his winter job when he managed in Elmira. There was one month in which he made seventeen sales. Earl can be persuasive—just ask his former customers or his players.

When Weaver became the Orioles' manager after the 1968 All-Star game, he posted this sign in the locker room: It Is What You Learn After You Know It All That Counts.

As much as anything else, that sums up Weaver's outlook. He believes he knows a lot about baseball, but he also knows that there is always more to learn: you can never have enough information.

While a minor-league manager, Weaver wrote the program for the entire Baltimore Orioles organization. He designed the drills, the cutoff plays, and the procedures for spring training. Every year he would add a new wrinkle. It really *is* what you learn after you know it all that counts.

Earl's clubs were a little different from other teams. For example, only one of Weaver's Oriole teams ever led the league in batting average. But they always outhomered their opponents. Hit home runs, but don't give them up.

The three-run homer is Weaver's weapon. Be patient. Wait for the big inning and the big rush to the top in the final months of the season.

Overall, Weaver had a .583 winning percentage with Baltimore. But after September 1 that mark was .602. His teams were like a well-trained marathoner. The 162-game season punishes the sprinter, who wilts in the July doubleheaders; a strong finish is what usually makes a pennant winner.

So Weaver's teams would often stumble out of the gate in April. Earl would be using all his players, getting each of them some work so they would be sharp when the games piled up and the entire twenty-five-man roster was needed. Perhaps that's why Weaver's teams won 65 percent of their games in doubleheader contests.

"If Earl Weaver has a player on his team, he will use him," says Orioles' general manager Hank Peters. "He does not believe in carrying anyone on the roster if he cannot contribute in some way."

Weaver scoffs at those who feel a team can bunt and steal a pennant. It might work in roomy parks like Kansas City or St. Louis, but the basic strategy is wrong. The length of a baseball game is measured in outs, and the bunt gives one away. Earl treasures each of the game's twenty seven-outs as if they were diamonds: none should be squandered.

Weaver's clubs made few errors and always executed fundamentals, a direct result of Earl's meticulously planned spring practices. They also drew a lot of walks; only one Weaver team failed to receive more bases on balls than its opponents. Once again, the key is patience. Wait for the pitch you can hit out of the park. If it doesn't come, take the walk down to first base so you can score if the next hitter gets *his* pitch.

Weaver also believes in the four-man pitching rotation. Most teams use five starters, but Earl feels that a fifth starter should be used only when a crowded schedule demands it. Odds are that the fifth starter is not as talented as the first four pitchers. So why take away starts from your four best hurlers to give them to your fifth?

"So much of baseball is plain old common sense," Earl insists. "I will never understand why some people don't want players to hit home runs. It's the greatest play in the game. And I don't understand why some people don't want to use their best pitchers as much as possible. If I'm managing, I like to have Jim Palmer, Mike Flanagan, and the other great pitchers on the mound. When they're out there, you know you've got a great chance to win."

The Orioles won a hundred games five times under Weaver. In fifteen major-league seasons, his clubs finished lower than second place just twice. Naturally, Weaver had plenty of talent with the Orioles, but when he became the Baltimore manager in 1968 the Birds were in sixth place. The year before they had finished in sixth with a 76–85 record. Weaver drove that '68 club up to second place. Then in each of the next three years he won over a hundred games. If he returns to managing, he can lose every game for three years and still have a career record over .500.

"Earl had plenty of good players," notes Brooks Robinson. "But he knew how to use them. Probably the best compliment I can give him is that other players would tell me that they wished Earl was in their dugout."

Weaver is perhaps best known for his clashes with umpires. In Rochester he grew weary of arguing with an umpire and simply picked up third base and carried it off the field and into the dressing room. While with the Orioles, he once carried a rule book onto the field and tore it up, demonstrating what he felt was the umpires' complete disregard for the rules.

"No one knows the rules better than Earl," says Harry Dalton. "The umpires may not like it, but they must respect him for it. He keeps them on their toes."

Earl was ejected from ninety-seven regular-season major-league games. He was also thrown out of an Instructional League game, a spring training game, and even a World Series game. In addition, he was suspended five times.

"The umpires are my best friends," says Weaver. "I'm not kidding. I don't believe they ever held anything against me, and I don't hold anything against them. They do the best they can. But when they made a mistake, I felt it was my job as the manager to let them know."

In 1982 Weaver was suspended for a week and fined $2,000 for making "physical contact with umpire Terry Cooney in an argument over a call at first base," according to a press release from American League president Lee MacPhail.

Weaver released his own statement on the suspension, and this part of it best reveals his attitude toward the umpires.

Lee MacPhail has again been kind enough to grant me seven days' vacation during the regular baseball season. The only thing unfair about this is that he gives his umpires two weeks during the year. Along with my time off he has also allowed me the chance to make a fine gain financially.

He is asking me to send him $2,000 in exchange for the long-needed rest. Consequently, with this extra time, I'll be able to make a few personal appearances and some television and radio spots that will increase the original investment some five to ten times.

Lee's kindness stems from an incident that occurred with umpire Terry Cooney last Saturday night. In Lee's eyes, Cooney and I made physical contact with each other and, as I looked at some film clips, it would be hard for me to say this didn't happen.

It's quite all right for an umpire to push and shove a baseball manager all over the field as clips from our highlight film will show you, but it's taboo for it to happen the other way around. These are the accepted rules in baseball, and I'm not going to be the one to argue against the rules. If there was physical contact, and the films seem to indicate there was, I am truthfully sorry.

Sunday, after the incident Saturday night, I called Terry Cooney and asked him if he would come to my office to discuss it. He proved to me that he is an outstanding individual by coming over and sitting down and talking about it with no anomosity *(sic)* or hateful revengeful feelings. He also went out that day and gave us one of the best games that we've had umpired all season long. . . . And this was after ejecting me from two straight ballgames. He built a lot of respect for himself in my eyes and again proves . . . that umpires have as much integrity as any working group of people anywhere.''

Earl has a sharp sense of humor, but he also has a deep respect for everyone in baseball—the front-office people, the scouts, the players, and the umpires. In fact, Weaver loved his players. After all, he wanted to be just like them when he signed his first pro contract at seventeen.

In the chapters that follow, Earl Weaver will tell you his approach to baseball. You will learn everything from how to break in a rookie pitcher through the bullpen to his prized first-and-third steal play. But most of all, you will learn what made Earl Weaver a winner.

TERRY PLUTO

December 1983

SPRING TRAINING

It May Be Boring,
But It Works

LET'S face it—spring training is pretty boring. But that doesn't mean it's not important.

There are three main purposes to spring training. First, the players need to condition their bodies and minds for the grind of a 162-game season. Second, I have to use the workouts and games to pick my twenty-five-man roster. Finally, the veteran players need to review fundamentals and the newcomers must learn my style of playing the game.

The worst type of spring training is a camp where nothing happens. You've got to make sure everybody's busy every minute they're on the field. Nothing is worse than wasted time. The players get bored and feel like they're not doing anything. The day drags on and on. Sure, sometimes the pitchers are going to have to stand around and shag balls during batting practice, but you try to keep even that to a minimum.

You can always have drills to keep people moving. All major-league clubs use two or three diamonds at a time in the spring. The Orioles train at Miami Stadium, and in the far corner of the park there's an extra infield, which we call the "little infield," though, of course, it's the usual size. There's no outfield behind it.

I always give a first-day speech in which I tell players, especially the young players, not to try and impress me by throwing too hard early in camp. That's a good way to get hurt, and it ends any chance a rookie has of making the club. If a player is injured, he can't display his ability. I worry about players coming from winter ball in Latin America; they think they're in shape, but that usually isn't the case. Often, they haven't done much for the three weeks between the end of the winter season and the start of spring training, and in that period they lose their edge. They too have to be careful not to get hurt.

I always tell my players that they must be somewhere doing something every minute of spring training. If they pay attention and follow directions, we'll get them off the field faster, because our work will be done. Again, I'm trying to keep standing around to a minimum. The first workout may only be ninety minutes, but the workouts get longer as the spring wears on.

The workouts are for the kids to learn my way of doing things. I was fortunate in that I was with the Orioles for fifteen years and my method was taught to them from the moment they signed with the club. I helped create the way of teaching fundamentals for the whole Baltimore system. A manager who is with a club for only two years doesn't have that luxury and has to spend even more time teaching.

First, you get the players in good physical shape. That isn't as difficult as it used to be. Today's players come to camp in much better condition than players did ten or twenty years ago. They've been on training programs during the winter—Nautilus, running, and so on. It makes the early part of camp a lot easier if a player arrives in shape. That's true for players on any level: you should always try to be in good condition when practice begins.

As a player, I went to one big-league spring training, with the St. Louis Cardinals in 1952. I was in shape. I had to be, because I was trying to earn a big-league job; I was twenty-one at the time and just thrilled to be in camp with the Cardinals. I was surprised to see that not all of the Cardinals were physically ready to play baseball. But back then veterans would come to camp planning to play themselves into shape. I remember seeing Enos Slaughter,

ON THE IMPORTANCE OF FUNDAMENTALS

People always say the Orioles had great "fundamentals" teams. That's true, but a lot of what they consider fundamentals is really just players having great talent.

A few years ago the Orioles were playing in Chicago. It was early in the season, and we had a 6–2 lead. I remember that it was a cold, miserable day. In the late innings the White Sox were starting to come back. They had a runner on first, and someone hit a ball into the gap in left-center field. The moment the ball left the bat I thought the runner from first would easily score.

Mark Belanger was playing shortstop, and he went into the outfield to take the cutoff throw from the fence. He caught the relay, turned, and uncorked a throw to the plate that went all the way from the outfield to the catcher about a foot off the ground. The runner was out at the plate, and the rally was over.

On the radio Chicago announcer Harry Caray was raving about the way Weaver's teams execute fundamentals. Actually, fundamentals didn't have much to do with it, because Belanger was the only guy who could make that type of play. I could teach fundamentals all my life and never show anyone how to make a play like that.

A manager can get the players in the right place and teach them where they are supposed to throw the ball, but they are the people who catch the ball, get rid of it in a split second, and throw it right on the money. That is talent, not managing.

who was a great ballplayer, with sweat pouring off him, working like a son of a gun to get the weight off. He would wear a rubber suit to help him sweat.

That's a terrible thing to do to your body, and besides, it's just not smart. Your career is only going to last so long. Baseball is a short life, and thirty-five is old for an infielder. Ballplayers especially have to keep their legs in shape. Once you get out of shape, you never return to your peak physical condition. It's impossible for you to get back to 100 percent. You can get in condition and maybe end up at 80 percent, but you'll never be the way you were the first time. Some players think they can get away with that, but they're cheating themselves and their teammates. That's something every ballplayer must remember, and that's why it's stupid to let yourself go in the off-season. You're just asking for trouble, risking your career and blowing a chance to make a lot of money.

I sincerely believe that today's players are more intelligent than the old-timers were. They realize that baseball is a short career, and they don't let themselves get fat in the winter. They also know that there are millions of dollars to be made in this game. These guys are smarter when it comes to taking care of their bodies. Well, most of them.

Often Boog Powell would weigh up to 300 pounds when he reported. I believe he held out a lot of springs just so he could get some of that weight off. He'd still come to camp a little overweight, but he was a throwback, a player who played himself into shape. Of course, sometimes you can go too far in the other direction, too. A few years ago Tim Stoddard went overboard. Stoddard is six feet seven inches tall and was a power forward on the North Carolina State basketball team. He's a big guy. With all good intentions he decided to drop some weight one winter, and he went from 270 to about 225 pounds. That was too much, and it made him weak. He didn't throw as hard. He had to work himself back up to 240, which is the right weight for him, and his fastball was much better.

I firmly believe that conditioning has a direct bearing on the length of a career. If you start at twenty-two or twenty-four years of age and keep in shape, you can play until you're thirty-eight or forty. Take Carl Yastrzemski. Before the 1967 season Yaz went on a strenuous and extremely demanding conditioning program. It paid off in two ways for him. First, he won the triple crown that year, so there was an immediate gain. But second, he has kept himself in that extraordinary shape and has produced year after year. The guy lasted into his forties and was still an outstanding hitter when most of the guys he broke into the majors with had been retired for years. Sure, Yaz has great talent. But he also isn't afraid of sweating and paying the price to stay in shape. It's easy to say "Keep in shape," but it requires a lot of effort. Frankly, there is no other way to do it, no short cuts. A player has to work hard every winter.

In spring training a manager wants to make sure that he gets his players in good condition. You don't want to rush them, because that's asking for injuries. Especially with pitchers.

Now, the Oriole pitchers throw over the winter. Many of them live in Baltimore, and they get together in the off-season. They usually throw three times a week off mounds in a special heated area under the grandstand at Memorial Stadium. That's a good idea, because the arm, like any other muscle, needs to be exercised. But in spring training, a manager must begin with the premise that his pitcher hasn't touched a ball all winter. He must make sure to stretch out their arms and have them ease into throwing. That first workout they'll throw five to seven minutes off a mound and they won't throw all out. During the next few days that moves up to ten minutes. Some guys will throw breaking balls, but they won't be sharp pitches. Mostly, they'll spin some curves just to get the feel of the pitch. A pitcher's fourth time on the mound will be his first batting practice outing.

Spring training means different things to different pitchers. Established pitchers like Jim Palmer use the spring to refine a certain pitch or perhaps work on the mechanics of their delivery. Palmer didn't have to worry about making the team; he could give up ten runs in two innings to the Red Sox and was still going to be my opening-day pitcher so long as he was healthy.

A rookie is in a different position. He has to show the manager that he has talent and that he can get people out in the majors. He doesn't have the luxury of getting bombed in Winter Haven. A terrible outing might get that kid sent back to Rochester.

It's hard to say how many openings there are on a staff each year, because there are so many variables. Usually no more than one or two rookie pitchers make the team. Some years none do. But if a kid has a lot of talent and he looks super just about every time he takes the mound in the spring, you're usually forced to find a spot for him. You can pitch your way onto a big-league team, but it isn't easy.

There are different schools of thought on how much a pitcher should throw. For example, Tommy John likes to throw all the time. I know that Ron Guidry, on the other hand, doesn't like to throw at all between starts. Jim Palmer will pitch, take a day off, and then throw between 120 and 140 pitches on the side the second day. He then takes the third day off and starts on the fourth day. (If Palmer were in a five-man rotation, he would rest for two days after his start, throw his 120 to 140 pitches on the third day, rest again on the fourth, and pitch on the fifth.) I think that throwing between starts is a good idea if the pitcher can do it. He can work on the things that may have caused him trouble in his last start. If the guy had problems with his curve, then he can try and fix that while throwing on the side. Also, the pitching coach can watch him and offer suggestions. If a pitcher gave up a lot of walks, he can smooth that out. He can throw to the catcher as if he were facing a hitter, going inside and up with one pitch and then low and away with the next. This is also a good opportunity for a pitcher to add another pitch.

For the most part pitchers' arms are in better shape today at the start of spring training than they were twenty years ago. The physical-fitness programs and the off-season throwing are the reasons. But remember the importance of money. Many of these guys now earn enough so that all they need to do is concentrate on baseball. Before the baseball-salary boom, guys had to work nine-to-five jobs in the winter, doing everything from driving a truck to being in a store. I suppose some rookies today have to work in the winter, but most realize the importance of off-season conditioning, and they make time to get it in. It's the only intelligent thing to do.

Another problem when pitchers aren't in shape is that they won't last as long on the mound. A pitcher can't give you nine innings unless he's in condition. I don't believe that there are teams that are in better shape than others year after year. That's basically out of the hands of the management. It is up to the individual player and how he wants to spend the off-season. You can't live with these guys all winter, and you can't force them to work out. But I'll say this: I could tell the minute a player walked into camp if he had done his work in the winter.

The best way to avoid injuries is to have good physical conditioning in spring training. Don't overdo it at the start, and work toward getting the players into the best shape possible. Gradually increase the number of laps and the severity of the exercises—that's the best way to avoid injuries.

Stretching exercises before a game are a good way to avoid those muscle pulls in the leg. A manager should stress the importance of stretching exercises. Not only is it crucial to be in good physical condition, but the players should stretch before every game to keep the body ready to play.

THE CLICHÉS OF SPRING

Another problem in spring camps is all those sportswriters with nothing much to write about. Every year it seemed I got asked the same questions, so I started giving my answers by the numbers. Here are my nine favorite answers.

1. *The hitters are ahead of the pitchers.* You use this one after your staff gets pounded for fourteen runs early in the spring. After all, maybe the hitters *are* ahead of the pitchers at this point. Who's to say which group develops faster?
2. *The pitchers are ahead of the hitters.* The opposite of number 1, so it should be used when you get shut out by three rookie pitchers nobody's ever heard of.
3. *The Second-Time-Out theory.* I'm not sure why it happens, but veteran pitchers often get hit in their second outing of the spring. When reporters asked me why, I had few answers. Instead, I'd just tell them it was just another case for the second-time-out theory.
4. *The Loss In Daytona Beach theory.* You can substitute any city, but this excuse is to be used when you get bombed on the road in the spring. So you lose to Montreal, 20–3, on March 22 in Daytona Beach. Who cares?
5. *That's why they call 'em exhibition games.* The Orioles often had records like 12–15 in the spring because I spent my time looking at players rather than worrying about winning. Most managers do the same. They call them "exhibition games" because they don't count.
6. *The Lee May syndrome.* This can be used for any veteran hitter who's having a lousy spring. Lee May couldn't hit his weight for me in the spring, but the man did the job once the season began. The writers would get nervous about Lee's springs, but I didn't worry. Guys who hit in the past and haven't gotten injured or too old are a great bet to hit again, regardless of their batting averages in Florida.

7. *Yes, Palmer will pitch the opener.* **Every spring it seemed that Jim Palmer had some sort of injury—elbow, back, ulna nerve, etc.— and people would wonder if Jim would be able to pitch the opener. There were millions of stories speculating about Palmer's condition. Usually Jim was ready when the bell rang. I never worried about it unless Jim came up to me right before the opener and said there was a problem.**

8. *Can't you see what we're doing out there?* **A lot of young writers had a million questions about what was happening in the spring. They didn't seem to understand that you had to do certain drills to get ready for the season. Rather than explain it all every day, it often was easier to pose this question. After all, they should have been smart enough to see what we were doing.**

9. *Phenom? What phenom?* **Every spring, the writers are looking for a phenom, a young player they can build up and go crazy about in their stories. I understand that they have to write something, but they've gotten carried away sometimes. I remember one rookie baseball writer who had Mark Corey ready for the Hall of Fame just because he hit the ball hard a couple of times in an intersquad game. Patience! It's a long way from the Grapefruit League.**

Early in spring training you have a lot of physical drills for your pitchers. You split them into groups, and one group works on covering first base on grounders to the right side of the infield. If a pitcher does that for twenty minutes, he gets a terrific workout. It's very demanding on a pitcher's legs, which are about as important to him as his arm.

While one group is working on covering first base, I'll have another group on the infield practicing their pickoff throws to first and second. The third group of pitchers will be in the outfield, shagging balls hit during batting practice. Jim Palmer loves to shag balls. He runs all over the place in the outfield: it's his way of keeping in shape. Jim does the same thing during the regular season before games. He loves to be in the outfield during batting practice. These three groups of pitchers rotate from one activity to the next over the course of the day. That adds a little variety, and they perfect their fundamentals at the same time.

For the camp to be worthwhile, everyone's got to be doing

something all day long. It's not hard to keep all this coordinated if a manager does his homework in the winter. I don't care if you are a high school coach, a college coach, or the manager of the Orioles, you must set up your program over the winter. If you don't have a plan, training camp can be chaotic.

Early in camp, start with pitchers and catchers and a few fundamentals. As the days move on, add more drills. Pickoffs are important, because the players really have to work together as a team. First, the catcher gives the pickoff sign and indicates where that pickoff throw goes. One method is for the catcher to put down a fist, which means the pickoff is on. He then puts down one finger, which means a throw to first. Two fingers could mean a throw to second. Since he gets the sign from the catcher, the pitcher never has to look at the base he's throwing to. After indicating the base, the catcher again puts his hand in a fist. The pitcher watches only the catcher's fist. When that fist opens, the pitcher whirls and throws to the appropriate base. It's a timing play, with the fielders also watching the catcher for the signals.

On the pickoff move to first base, you can sometimes cheat a little. Certain umpires will not call balks. The pitcher can twist his shoulder halfway to the clubhouse and they won't call a thing. You add a little "cheat" move to a pitcher's repertoire and tell your pitcher that he can use it when certain umpires are at first base. It doesn't mean a balk *won't* be called, but you can get away with it most of the time. I know of an umpire who has called only one balk in his career. He told me this, and he said he only called the balk because the pitcher dropped the ball while on the mound, and that's an automatic balk. Furthermore, the umpire said he waited until the ball bounced twice before making the call.

Every player in the majors should be able to perform fundamentals. But as with everything else, some are better at it than others. Some people are smarter than others and pick up on these signs and do a better job of keeping them straight.

Even before camp begins, a manager is working. In addition to setting up his spring program he's got to familiarize himself with the new players coming to camp. You may have over forty guys in camp, and ten to fifteen of them are rookies, guys you've never seen before. I'd spend the winter going over our scouting reports, studying the rookies' minor-league records, and talking to some scouts. I wanted all the information I could get on them. That way I'd have an idea of what to look for. Say I had a report from one of our minor-league managers that a certain young pitcher was as fast as Jim Palmer. Well, you'd better believe I'd keep my eye out for that kid.

During the winter you go over your roster with the general manager and begin to decide what players to watch the most. But some players surprise you. In the spring of 1979 Sammy Stewart didn't figure to make the team. Oh, we knew he had potential and a damn good arm. Our pitching coach, Ray Miller, had handled Sammy in the minors and really liked him, but we already had a strong staff, and we figured he was a year or two away. But that spring Sammy looked good at every opportunity. He allowed one run in seventeen spring innings. We had the radar gun on him, and he was throwing well over 90 miles an hour. There was no choice: we had to make room for him on the ballclub. With the kind of pitching we had in 1979, we didn't believe a young pitcher like Sammy would break in, but the man was throwing 92 miles an hour, and those guys are few and far between. He was a little wild, but that can sometimes help a hard-thrower—it's damn hard for a hitter to get around on a fastball when he's worried about having to duck.

Another player who forced us to keep him when we weren't sure that he was ready for the majors was Eddie Murray. In the spring of 1977 Eddie's highest level of experience had been 54 games at our Class AAA club in Rochester, New York. During the winter we got great reports on the way Murray was playing in Puerto Rico. We knew he had a lot of talent, but he had just turned twenty-one at the start of camp.

Well, that winter just about every team in baseball approached us about getting Eddie Murray in a trade. With all that background I knew that Eddie Murray was a guy I wanted to see swing the bat. Generally speaking, Murray is not a good batting-practice hitter. He saves his best swings for the game. But in the spring of 1977 Eddie knew that he had to concentrate on batting practice if he was going to make the team. I also made sure that I watched Eddie closely during batting practice. Well, his swing was beautiful from both sides of the plate. A switch-hitter is a great thing. Eddie had learned to switch-hit before the 1976 season. He was a natural right-handed hitter, and the change really helped his chances. I was very impressed that a player who had been switch-hitting for only a year seemed so natural from either side of the plate.

In batting practice Eddie was awesome. So I knew that I had to see this guy in some spring games. In one of the first exhibition games in which he appeared, Eddie went five for five, all shots, one over the center-field fence. I kept using him, and he kept hitting. Sometimes these situations are very simple. You let the guy play his way *off* the club. Eddie never did, because he kept hitting. He showed no weaknesses.

What made this decision a little tougher was that we had Lee May as our starting first baseman. In 1976 Lee had hit 25 homers and knocked in a league-leading 109 runs for me. Lee was thirty-four at the time, but he had hit at least twenty homers in each of the previous nine seasons. He was like money in the bank, good for about twenty-five homers and almost a hundred RBIs a year. There aren't too many players around like that. In the field, I was satisfied with Lee at first base: he had made only three errors in ninety-four games.

Eddie had been a first baseman in the minors. I tried him a little in the outfield, but that didn't work out. After all is said and done, Eddie has turned out to be a much better first baseman than Lee. Eddie has more range and a better arm, and he is quicker. But at that time I was still very happy with Lee. Also, I didn't want to put Eddie in there at first base and have him make a couple of errors early in the season. You never know how a rookie will react to his first taste of the majors. I could have been wrong; perhaps Eddie would never have made those errors, but I decided to keep Lee at first and use Eddie as our designated hitter in 1977. (In 1976 I had used several players as the DH—Pat Kelly, Terry Crowley, Andres Mora, and sometimes Lee May.) So Eddie became our full-time DH and Lee stayed at first. I just didn't want a situation early in the season in which Eddie might make an error or two and then have everybody say, "Why the hell doesn't Weaver have May at first?" Why put Eddie under that extra pressure if you don't have to?

It soon became obvious to everyone that Eddie had what you

want in a first baseman—the great hands, arm and agility. He was
a natural, and the following year he was at first and Lee was the
DH.

During spring games, you watch the individual performances
very closely. You can't take spring games too seriously.

WEAVER'S FIRST LAW

No one's going to give a damn in July if you lost a game in March.

There are some veterans, especially the big swingers, who are
bad spring hitters. Boog Powell and Lee May are two that come to
mind. But you know what they have done for you in the past, so
you don't worry about how they hit in Miami. What counts is the
way they hit the ball in Baltimore, New York, and Cleveland.
Powell often had bad Aprils. He couldn't stand the cold weather.
He would go into May hitting around .100, but you had to stick
with Boog until he got going.

On the other side of the coin is a guy like Pat Kelly. He would
walk into training camp and hit line drives the first time he stepped
into a batting cage. I don't know why, but Pat often would be
leading the league in hitting around May 15. Kelly always was a
good hitter, but he was especially hot in the early season, and a
manager should pay attention to such trends and get that guy in
the lineup whenever possible in April and May. Kelly and John
Lowenstein hit the ball as well the first day in camp as they do in
June.

If a rookie has a bad spring training, he's going back to the
minors. That's just the way of baseball. Young players don't get
the benefit of the doubt, and they have to show something in spring
training to make the roster.

Once the season starts, it's a different matter. You've got to
have some faith in your judgment. I've had rookies slump and I've
stuck with them. In 1982 Cal Ripken, Jr., was batting .089 going
into May. It was getting close to the point that he might have to be

sent back to the minors. But then he got hit by a pitch, and I kept him out of the lineup for a few extra days, just to let him sit for a while and get things in perspective. He got back into the lineup and never came out again, won Rookie-of-the-Year, and was one of the keys to our stretch drive. In 1977 Rich Dauer started the season at one for forty-four, and we were losing. General manager Hank Peters came to me and said that we didn't have to keep Rich in the majors. I said, let's give him a little more time. That year I had Dauer going in and out of the lineup, alternating with Billy Smith. We could afford to keep Dauer on because Billy Smith was hitting and doing well in the field. Eventually Dauer emerged as one of the best second basemen in the American League. Even though Mike Flanagan started one season at 2–8, I kept him in the rotation. It comes down to baseball knowledge, your believing that these guys can perform and win games for you. But it takes patience, and that's tough when you're losing. When those guys aren't producing, they're losing games for you. You weigh that every day you come to the park. If you stay too long with the players who aren't producing and aren't doing the job, you get fired.

In spring training, the most important job for a manager is picking his twenty-five players. I don't buy the saying that a manager wins his games by the way he picks his players in the spring and tries not to lose them in July. That's an overstatement, but the composition of the roster is obviously crucial. The general manager and I would talk once a week during the spring. We'd spend a lot of that time discussing—haggling over, almost—the final roster. Naturally I wanted the twenty-five best ballplayers, but it doesn't always work that way.

The manager's job is to win. The GM wants to win, too, but he has other, long-term problems to worry about. Once a player makes it to a big-league camp, he has three minor-league "options"; that is, he can be sent to the minors and recalled any number of times for three years. For example, the Yankees recalled and sent Steve Balboni back to their Class AAA club in Columbus several times in 1983, but that only counted as one option because it all took place during one season. After the player's three options are up, a decision must be made; if he's farmed out for a fourth time, he becomes a "frozen" player and can't be

A ROOKIE'S GUIDE TO MAKING A CLUB

1. *Concentrate and execute the drills.* Every great player I've managed
   —Frank Robinson, Brooks Robinson, Jim Palmer, Eddie Murray,
   Mark Belanger, and the rest—executed our fundamental drills with
   enthusiasm and care each spring. They did it the same way the
   tenth year as they did it the first—and these are players who could
   execute fundamentals in their sleep. They never let down or forgot
   the importance of drills.
2. *Hit with power.* Hitting the ball a long way is a quick way to catch
   someone's eye. A manager never has enough home-run hitters. In
   his first spring, Eddie Murray grabbed my attention by the way he
   hit the ball in batting practice.
3. *Throw hard.* You don't want a rookie hurting himself by overex-
   tending his arm, but every manager is on the lookout for a good
   fastball. Sammy Stewart is a good example.
4. *Be in shape.* A rookie doesn't have the luxury of playing himself
   into condition. He must make an impression right from the start.
   Therefore, he should be in peak physical and mental condition when
   he reports to camp.
5. *Show some speed.* This is a God-given talent. Either you can run or
   you can't. The player with outstanding speed who knows how to use
   it on the bases will get a good look.
6. *Watch the veterans.* They know how to act, and they know what is
   expected. Eddie Murray learned a lot from Lee May. The veterans
   have been through camp before, and a rookie can pick up a lot from
   them.
7. *Be patient.* Even if you are farmed out, you could end up back in
   the majors. Play well in the minors and you can't be ignored. It's a
   long season, and there are injuries, trades, and other things that
   will force a team to look to the minors for help. Just ask Mike
   Boddicker.

recalled unless he passes irrevocable waivers. That means that every team has a crack at drafting him for $25,000 before you can get him to your club. When some players are out of minor-league options, you want to keep them on the big-league club rather than send them back to Rochester and have them frozen all year and then be available to another club in the winter minor-league draft.

Sometimes a player is like a piece of property you can't get rid of. There may be a veteran the general manager wants you to hang on to until a trade can be made. Obviously, you can't go and throw $400,000 ballplayers out the window for nothing even if they can't help your team. That's bad business. But on the other hand, if you have too many players on the roster only because you can't trade them or farm them out, it's going to cost you dearly. If you lose, no one comes through the gate; that's bad business, too. So you try to strike a balance.

You need someone for each job that needs to be done when the time arises. In spring training, I'll look for a guy who can pinch-hit, a guy who can pitch in middle relief, maybe a player who can go out to the outfield for late-inning defense. When I was looking at Gary Roenicke, a right-handed hitter, to play in left field, I wanted someone else to be there in case Gary didn't hit. In this instance, we had John Lowenstein, a left-handed hitter. Lowenstein is worth his weight in gold: he can play all three outfield positions and some third base, he hits for power, and he knows his job. He's always ready when you need him, and he's a perfect player for anyone's bench.

The ideal situation is to have nine guys who can hit, run, throw, and field at each position. Then you can use one lineup every day. Well, hell, that doesn't exist—ever. Even good players run into a pitcher they simply can't hit. For example, Gary Roenicke may never hit Dan Quisenberry. Boog Powell was one for sixty-one against Mickey Lolich. You defeat your purpose when you have guys in the lineup against pitchers they can't hit. Boog had a miserable time against Jim Kaat, too. So when Lolich or Kaat pitched, it wasn't smart to have Powell in the lineup. The fact that he is Boog Powell won't help you win that particular game against that particular pitcher. You're fighting overwhelming odds.

For the bench, I look for a guy who can do a job when I want it done. Naturally I'm looking for as many talents as possible in one player. But your all-around players—those who can hit, run, and throw—are usually your regulars. On the bench you get guys with one excellent skill, a guy who can hit certain types of pitchers, for example. By matching your bench-players' strengths to your starters' weaknesses, you can create a "player" of All-Star caliber from spare parts. In 1982 we used Benny Ayala, John Lowenstein, and Gary Roenicke in left field. They combined to hit 37 homers, which is the same as having a Reggie Jackson in the batting order. Individually, Roenicke, Lowenstein, or Ayala could never compare to Jackson, but when used against the pitchers they could hit, they collectively performed like a star.

Veterans end up on the bench more often than rookies because they can mentally handle playing part-time better than most rookies. But I don't necessarily think that it's bad to have rookies on the bench. Some people believe in sending a rookie back to the minors for the kid's sake if he isn't going to start. But why not keep him on the roster if he can help you win? A young player may be able to play twice a week and help you win two games. That amounts to eight a month, or forty-eight games a year. Of course, if a kid is just sitting and rotting on the bench, you have to send him back to the minors. But if a rookie is ever going to be a big leaguer, someone has to give him a chance in the majors. That doesn't necessarily mean playing him every day. I've always believed in using the whole bench, and I know that if a kid gets a chance to play and has the talent, he will come through.

WEAVER'S SECOND LAW

If you don't make any promises to your players, you won't have to break them.

Most players are broken in gradually. No one is handed the job. A manager can't afford to make a firm commitment to a player. You simply cannot say that some kid is going to play the first fifty or sixty games. If you lose forty of those games, you're out of a job. If for the sake of the team you take the kid out of the lineup, you've lied to him. You shouldn't tell a rookie anything.

I try not to say a word to a rookie. When he makes the team out of spring training, I usually just tell him to pack his bags and come up north with us. I say I don't know how much he will play, and that we'll have to see what happens. I tell a rookie the same thing when he is promoted from the minors during the season. Never make a promise you can't keep.

Cutting a ballplayer is the toughest job for any manager, because you are giving him some of the worst news of his life. It hurts him, and it bothers you. But it's an obligation, a part of the job. Try to tell a player exactly why he didn't make the team, even though the player probably won't believe you. Few of them believe what you're saying; their opinion of their talent is different from yours.

Sometimes a kid has a great spring, but you send him back to the minors because you are sticking with the veterans. In 1980 and 1981 Drungo Hazewood always led our team in homers and hitting, but we didn't think he was ready for the majors. I can't say for certain that Hazewood would not have helped the Orioles, but he went back to the minors and didn't produce. Of course, getting cut after a good spring can break a player's spirit. It shouldn't, but it happens.

What you tell a player when you cut him is, go down to the minors and make me bring you back; force my hand. If a player goes to Triple-A and has a good season, some other club will take him if you don't bring him to the majors. The player controls his own destiny more than most realize.

When I was cut, I was happy just to play ball someplace. That's not the right attitude. It's better when a player tells his manager that he'll be back because the team is going to need him. He should tell himself, "I'm going to play in the major leagues." All I said was that I wanted to play, but believe me, a player is much better off sitting on a big-league bench than starting in the minors. As long as you're in the majors, that chance to play will come, and then you can make the most of it.

I broke in over a hundred rookies, all of the Oriole players for fifteen years. Murray, Dauer, Bobby Grich, Don Baylor, Al Bumbry—all of them got their starts under me. Some say that I didn't do well handling rookies, but look at the players I broke in. They had the talent, but I gave them the chance.

Bobby Grich and Don Baylor both went back to the minor leagues with the right attitude. They were rookies in camp after we had won three straight pennants, from 1969 to 1971. I farmed Grich out after he had batted .383 at Rochester with eight homers. He went back to the minors and hit .336 with 32 homers. Grich forced us to make a spot for him: we traded our starting second baseman, Dave Johnson, to Atlanta that winter.

From the start of my managerial career, I was pretty sure of my baseball judgment. I felt I could size up a player well and know whether or not he could play. Of course, in the low minors it is even tougher to cut a guy, because when you do you're usually releasing him. It's one thing to be sent back to the minors, and a whole other ballgame to get a ticket home. But you've still got to go with your best judgment, no matter how much it might hurt somebody.

Players and managers come and go, but the drills stay the same. You can add a new wrinkle here or there, but it's the same damn game. There's no way you can change a pitcher covering first base or a pitcher throwing to first base.

The following are a couple of the things we would work on every spring that form the heart of the famous "Oriole Fundamentals."

Cutoff Plays

When you practice cutoffs from the outfield, the whole team goes on the field. This had to be terribly boring for Frank Robinson, Brooks Robinson, Mark Belanger—the veterans who could do it in their sleep. But they set the tone for the camp. They were enthusiastic and worked hard at it. The rookies would see this and realize that practicing these fundamentals was important. They'd say, "If Brooks pays attention and performs them with care, then I should do it that way, too." I was fortunate because the veterans realized that we had ten to fifteen new people in camp each year who needed to learn these fundamentals, so they set a good example.

Cutoffs vary from team to team, depending on the players involved. This is where a manager has to know the ability of his athletes. Usually the first baseman will be the cutoff man on throws to the plate from right field and center field. But there was one team in the league that had the third baseman handle all the throws—the first baseman was so slow, he had a tough time getting into position. Normally the third baseman would handle only the throws from left to home.

For balls hit in the alleys—left-center and right-center—you should send out your best arm for the relay, whether it's the second baseman or the shortstop. The other player then covers second base.

Rundowns

Eddie Stanky used to have a drill with a runner on third and less than two outs. Say the ball was hit hard right to the shortstop and the man was running from third to home on the play. The runner knew he would be out at home plate, so Stanky wanted him to get in a rundown so that the man who hit the ground ball could get to second base. Stanky was 100 percent right in wanting his players to stay in a rundown as long as possible. He also asked his players to hit the ground at the fielder's feet just as he was about to be tagged out. This way, the man with the ball would fall over the runner and be unable to make a throw. The trouble is, the man getting tagged is risking an injury. I would worry if Eddie Murray got in a rundown, fell down, and then had the catcher step on his hand, knocking him out of action for three weeks. It's a smart play, but it sure can backfire. You need your best players on the field day in and day out.

When our runners make a mistake, I want to keep them in a rundown as long as possible. But what I am far more concerned about is defending against this play. If the rundown is executed correctly, the runner can be tagged out with one throw and the other player can't take the extra base. This is so simple that it's unbelievable that major leaguers mess it up. Suppose we are playing the Yankees and they have a runner on third with one out. The New York hitter slaps a grounder to Rich Dauer at second. Dauer fields the ball and sees that the runner on third is breaking for the plate. Dauer fires the ball to the catcher. At the same time, *our third baseman must trail the runner down the line.* The moment our catcher gets the ball, the runner stops, hoping to get in a rundown. But if you do it right, the third baseman is right behind the runner. The catcher throws to the third baseman, who puts the quick tag on the runner. Meanwhile, the guy who hit the ground ball doesn't have time to get to second base. Timing is all-important. The third baseman has to know to trail the runner, and that's the type of thing that spring training is all about.

Pitchers' Fielding Drills

Some pitchers have trouble learning to field their position. Say there's a runner on first and a ground ball is hit back to the mound. This should be a double play if the pitcher keeps his cool. The key is for the pitcher not to separate his hands. By that I mean he should get the ball in his glove and keep his bare hand in the glove until he is ready to throw. The mistakes come when the pitcher takes the ball out of his glove too early and holds the ball behind him, ready to throw it before his fielders are ready to cover second base. Most wild throws come when the pitcher's arm is cocked for too long; when he finally brings it forward, he can't stop himself from firing it into center field. But if the pitcher keeps the ball in his glove until he sees who's at second and *then* takes the ball out of his glove, he will make a good throw. This is something we work on in spring training until the pitchers have it coming out of their eyes. Things like this can make a big difference in those one-run games.

Once in a while—and it shouldn't be too often—no one covers second. Sometimes a pitcher just stands there and doesn't know what to do. So during spring training when I'm standing by second base, I'll sometimes have no one cover the bag. That way the pitcher knows to keep his composure and at least get the runner at first.

Bunt Defenses

Man on first: The first baseman has two options on a bunt play: he can either charge right toward the bunter immediately, or he can take two steps toward home and then retreat back to the bag for a pickoff throw, forcing the runner to return to first. There is a sign for each play so that the pitcher isn't delivering to home plate while the first baseman is on his way back to the bag. There might also be a sign for throwing to first base twice, then going home.

As the pitch is thrown, the third baseman should be on top of the hitter. The first baseman and pitcher also charge. The second baseman covers first, the shortstop covers second, and the catcher covers third.

Runners on first and second: The normal play is for the third baseman to stay near the bag, with the pitcher covering balls bunted toward third. Sometimes, the Orioles would have the third baseman charge the hitter, with the shortstop covering third, the second baseman covering second, and the first baseman staying close to the bag so he can cover it. The pitcher covers the right side of the infield. On this play, the third baseman has to chase the pitcher off the ball.

A variation of mine on this play was to field the bunt, wheel, and throw to second for one out and then have the second baseman relay to first for a double play. Sometimes you can catch the runners by surprise because they assume you're only going for a play at third. This different type of double play would work three or four times a year. On this play, I always have every base covered; a few big-league teams leave second base open.

Defending against the Steal with Runners on First and Third

The catcher is the most important person in this play. When the runner breaks from first base to second, the catcher must look at third before throwing to second. A good look at the runner on third will usually stop him. Then the catcher can throw to second. Experience has proven that if the catcher stops the runner on third with a glance, there is no way he can start up again and be able to score. The relay from the second baseman or shortstop will nail him at the plate every time. If the catcher sees the runner about twenty feet off third base, that runner is ready to be picked off. Then the catcher simply throws to the third baseman and the runner is run down and tagged out.

That look the catcher gives the runner at third base may take an extra second, making it a little tougher for the catcher to throw out the guy streaking for second base. But the catcher still has enough time to get all but the super base stealers. So he can't throw out a Rickey Henderson. Well, no one can throw out Henderson if he has a good jump from first base. The key is the look to freeze the runner on third.

THE OFFENSE

Praised Be the Three-Run Homer!

SOME PEOPLE ask me why I was so reluctant to use the bunt. I guess they don't think there's anything more to managing than filling out the lineup card and deciding when to bunt.

Well, I've got nothing against the bunt—in its place. But most of the time that place is the bottom of a long-forgotten closet.

Forget about the bunt unless there is no other choice. Look instead to Dr. Longball and his assistant, Dr. Three-Hit. Those are the best friends of any manager, and they can make a team healthy in a hurry.

The home run makes managing simple. Frank Robinson would come to bat with two guys on base. I'd yell, "Hit it hard, Frank." Frank would hit it hard and far, over the fence. Then he would come around the bases and back into the dugout. I'd say, "Nice hit, Frank." Now *that* is the ideal way to manage, and that's how people first decided I was smart. Of course, you've got to have the guys who can hit the ball over the wall. Give me a lineup full of Frank Robinsons, Eddie Murrays, and Brooks Robinsons, and I'll show you how simple managing can be.

The home run is my favorite subject. It's the most exciting play in baseball—the sport's knockout punch. It's often the difference between winning and losing. Finally, it's one of the reasons for the success of the Baltimore Orioles.

In my mind, the home run is paramount, because it means instant runs. The minute you hit a homer you have a run, no questions asked. With anything else, you aren't guaranteed a run. Sure, you can hit something other than a homer with a man on base and drive in a run; but hit a homer with a runner on and you have two runs. On a home run, nothing can go wrong. You can't be robbed by a fielder making a great catch or by your baserunner falling down or by someone being thrown out. Why people can't see that, I'll never know. Some people seem to be amazed to hear that home runs win games, when it's the most obvious thing in the world. Look at Babe Ruth and Lou Gehrig. A big reason those Yankee teams were so great in the 1920s and 1930s was that they hit the ball out of the park. "Murderer's Row." The power of the home run is so elementary that I fail to comprehend why people try to outsmart this game in other ways. If I were to play a singles hitter in right field or left field or at third base, he'd have to hit well over .300 and get on base often to be as valuable as a twenty-five-homer man.

WEAVER'S THIRD LAW

The easiest way around the bases is with one swing of the bat.

There are many coaches who believe in teaching players to swing for singles. That's OK for some guys, but not everybody. As a hitting coach, Charlie Lau is known for producing .300 hitters, and he has turned out a number of them. But when Charlie was with a team that hit a lot of homers, they won. When he was with singles-hitting clubs, they lost.

I see nothing wrong with telling those who have the ability to try and hit home runs. A manager must always remember his players' capabilities and incapabilities and never ask a player to do something that is beyond him. But if you have a young man who is strong, then he should try to supply some power. When Don Baylor came up to the Orioles in 1972, hitting 10–12 homers with his strength and talent, I talked to him about looking to hit the 2–0 and 3–1 pitches out of the park. It took a little time, but he eventually became the 25–30 home run man I knew he could be.

The secret to hitting is to look for a certain pitch in a certain area of the strike zone, and that's true whether you're Mark Belanger or Don Baylor. Mark may only be able to hit that pitch for a single, while Baylor can hit it over the fence. But if a hitter looks for a certain pitch in a certain area and then gets it, he should hit the ball hard. After that it depends on his physical attributes; a strong guy puts it over the wall, and a weaker hitter maybe lines it over second base.

Ted Williams was the greatest hitter who ever lived. Some say he was a guess hitter because he was usually looking for a certain pitch in a certain area. In fact, Williams would divide the plate up into sections according to which was the best area to swing at a certain pitch. I think *guessing* is the wrong word; it's better to say you're *looking for* something. You may believe the pitcher is going to give you a certain pitch based on any number of factors—the count, what he has thrown you before—so it isn't a blind guess at all. It's using your head.

As is so often true in baseball, the ball-strike count plays a big part. If the hitter is ahead in the count, he should look for that certain pitch in a certain area. If the hitter gets a different pitch, he shouldn't swing. Otherwise, he's just wasting his advantage.

A hitter must be intelligent enough to know who's pitching and what that guy usually throws. You can help the hitter by reminding him of some things, but he's got to be able to do it for himself, too. Time and time again some hitters swing at a pitch they can't handle, a pitch that may even have been out of the strike zone. It comes down to patience and intelligence. Ted Williams would walk 130 times a year and drive in 130 runs. He got criticized for not swinging at pitches close to the plate, but Williams never would have been such a great hitter if he felt he had to swing at the pitcher's pitch. He would have been playing right into the pitcher's hands.

It all starts before the game. Say Fergie Jenkins is the pitcher that night. Jenkins throws his slider 75 percent of the time. A good, smart hitter knows he is going to see the slider, and there's no way around that fact. But the hitter should make sure he swings at sliders in the strike zone. If Jenkins doesn't throw the slider over, the hitter doesn't swing. It sounds simple, but it takes practice. Jenkins has struck out hundreds of hitters on sliders outside the strike zone. It's a very tough pitch to take, and that's why Jenkins has struck out some three thousand batters. If Jenkins threw ten straight fastballs, the hitter would be gone, completely fooled. But the odds are overwhelmingly against getting ten fastballs from Jenkins. A hitter is far more likely to see five straight sliders. A hitter also has to be realistic against Jenkins, because he makes few mistakes. Usually, he keeps the slider outside and at the knees to a right-handed hitter. If that batter is trying to pull the ball, he may as well stay home. You can only hit that low-and-away pitch up the middle or to right field. Once in a while, Jenkins will hang a pitch, and that is what a hitter can pull—but those mistakes are rare.

Ballplayers should know their pitchers. A manager should make a point of letting a rookie hitter know what to look for against a certain pitcher, but most veteran hitters don't need reminders. If they did, they wouldn't last long enough to be veterans.

The radar gun can be a big help. It enables you to know exactly how hard a pitcher is throwing. Knowledge like that eliminates the sneaky fastball. The Orioles were the first team in the majors to make extensive use of the radar gun, and I love it. It's another tool that gives a manager information. It took me six years to convince the front office that we should have the guns in our minor-league system, but I believe most baseball people acknowledge that a radar gun is a good investment, even though one costs over fifteen hundred dollars. The first thing the Baltimore hitters want to know about an opposing pitcher is his radar-gun reading. The hitters also want to know the difference between the speed of his changeup and the speed of his fastball. That helps them to know what to expect. Of course, we also use it on our own pitchers. When a pitcher is throwing at 88 miles an hour most of the game and then goes to the mound in the eighth inning and is at 84 miles an hour, it is a good bet that he's tiring.

The man who operates the radar gun at Baltimore's Memorial Stadium sits behind the plate. He relays the pitchers' speeds to the people in the dugout through hand signals. We tried walkie-talkies, but there was too much interference. I would have liked to take someone with us on the road to run the radar gun, but the club thought the expense was too great. But sometimes a little knowledge like that is enough of an edge to win you some ballgames.

Because it's so difficult to know for sure what kind of pitch they'll see and where it'll be thrown, the best hitters succeed only three of every ten times. The pitcher has the advantage, because he knows what he will throw. The hitter can only make an educated guess.

Say you're facing Tommy John. Right away, you know that he doesn't throw hard. Second, you know he gives up a lot of ground balls, so he throws a lot of sinkers. Third, if you watch him for a few innings, you'll see that he gets hitters to swing at pitches that are low in the strike zone. So now you know what to look for; odds are the pitch will be a sinker, and you shouldn't worry about anything else.

On the other hand, a guy like Ron Guidry throws really hard and has a mean slider. He also has a change-up, but that definitely is his third pitch. So you'd better have a quick bat. While Tommy John doesn't throw much over 80 miles an hour, Guidry will be around 90. Believe me, there is a huge difference between 80 and 90 miles an hour.

Bert Blyleven has one of the best curves in baseball, and he will throw it to both right-handed and left-handed hitters. You can't just sit on Blyleven's curve, because he also has a fine fastball. Nevertheless, when you face Blyleven you must be aware of the curveball, because odds are you will see it at some point.

There's one ballpark in the American League where it would be a mistake to try and go with power, and that's Kansas City. If I managed the Royals, I would have to go for speed over power. Willie Aikens would be hitting thirty homers a year for anyone else, but the deep fences in Royals Stadium eat him up. That park would eat up the Orioles whenever we played there: our record against Kansas City was horrendous, and speed was the reason. They had a very fast team in the field and we didn't. On that Tartan Turf and with the deep fences, it made a big difference. Their hitters swing down on the ball and hit it through the infield. The K.C. infielders play exceptionally deep, maybe three steps back on what would be the outfield grass at a normal park. That takes away a lot of hits, and they can play so far back because they're fast enough to charge in and handle the high chops in time to get the Orioles' runners at first. But if our infielders played that far back, it wouldn't work because of the Royals' speed down to first. Frank White, Willie Wilson, George Brett, and some of the others could hit ground balls right at our infielders and still beat the throw.

In Kansas City, the Orioles looked terrible. Our lack of team speed would show us up. Our fly balls, which would be out of most parks, would get caught on the warning track. It was awful. Their speed beat us at every turn. Because of it, our outfielders had to play deeper on the artificial turf to stop the ball from scooting through to the wall for triples or inside-the-park home runs. That meant a lot of balls fell in front of them for hits. The speed of the Royals' outfielders enabled them to play shallower. So, once again, they were getting to the balls we couldn't reach.

In the rest of the parks in the American League, power is the way to go. There are differences; with that short left-field wall in Boston, they should have right-handed power hitters. The close right-field wall in Yankee Stadium means a team should have plenty of strong left-handed hitters.

But you've got to remember that while you play eighty-one games at home, you play another eighty-one in other parks. You've got to build for your home park, but you've got to have other weapons so you can win on the road, too. But in Kansas City you do need that speed. If I managed the Royals, I'd steal more bases. You can't sit and wait for the three-run homer there. A manager has to adjust to his club. Generally speaking, most major-league teams can be built around power, because most of the stadiums are not like the one in Kansas City.

The Bunt: Rarely Worth the Trouble

Its name, the sacrifice bunt, tells you something. *Sacrifice* means you are giving up something. In this instance, you're giving up an out to the opposition. There are only three an inning, and they should be treasured. It's such a basic fact that fans sometimes forget it, but an inning doesn't last fifteen minutes or six batters or twenty pitches; it lasts three outs. Give one away and you're making everything harder for yourself.

WEAVER'S FOURTH LAW

Your most precious possessions on offense are your twenty-seven outs.

You have to know that the one or two runs you're bunting for will win the game. If not, it doesn't make much sense to bunt. Bunting in the second or third inning is beyond me. No one alive knows that early in the game if his pitcher is only going to give up one or two runs or five runs. Stats will tell you that a pitcher with a 2.50 ERA will need fewer runs to win than one with a 5.50 ERA. It also tells you that it isn't bright to bunt for a run or two in the game with the 5.50-ERA pitcher on the mound for you. Do that, and you'll wind up on the short end most of the time. And even your best pitcher has some games where he needs all the runs you can get for him.

WEAVER'S FIFTH LAW

If you play for one run, that's all you'll get.

The object is to use the bunt when it will win the game. Another consideration is the batter: Can he drive in the run by swinging the bat, or is he a player who leaves them on base? Is it Mark Belanger or Eddie Murray? Use Belanger to bunt a runner over. But why bunt with Murray or Frank or Brooks Robinson?

I'm not sure there is as much bunting as people believe. Certainly fans talk about bunting more than it actually happens. My outlook on the bunt has never changed: it's an out you're giving the opposition, and no one is even certain that the bunt will be successful. A player can pop up the pitch or bunt it to the wrong part of the field. However, if it's the ninth inning and the score is tied and there's a runner on first and no outs, you should usually bunt him to second. That's an instant-win situation. But make sure you use your head about the hitter.

Does a guy like Eddie Murray drive in more runners from first base than many other players drive in from second? I bet he does, especially if he is hitting his thirty homers. In fact, Eddie often drives in a man from home plate—when he hits the ball out of the park. That's another thing you must consider before you have a power hitter bunt. In 1982 Benny Ayala and John Lowenstein were hitting homers for me about every fourteen times up. That meant that every fourteen at bats those two players were doing a hell of a lot to win me a game. That makes you think twice about having them bunt.

Here's another problem with the bunt: Say it's the ninth inning, the score is tied, and Rich Dauer leads off with a walk. Ken Singleton is the hitter, and Eddie Murray is on deck. I could have Singleton sacrifice Dauer to second, and then Murray would come to the plate with a chance to win the game with a single. But if I have Singleton bunt, the other team will intentionally walk Murray. By bunting, I've taken the bat out of the hands of my two best hitters. It sounds silly, but it happens all the time, with both the bunt and the hit-and-run.

Even in the late innings, I don't like to bunt with a runner on second and no outs. Say it's the ninth inning and Al Bumbry leads off with a double. Some would say I should bunt Bumbry to third so he could score on a sacrifice fly. It sounds good, but if Bumbry is sacrificed to third, the opposing manager could intentionally walk my next two hitters to load the bases. Then, the inning could be over on one pitch if my batter hits into a double play. All it would take to end the threat would be one good low fastball from the pitcher.

Another factor to consider about bunting a runner to third base is that it's no cinch to hit a sacrifice fly. In fact, it is pretty damn hard, particularly when the pitcher knows that run will beat him. There are more singles and doubles hit with a runner on third than sacrifice flies, and most of these will score a guy from second, too. The guy who leads the league in sacrifice flies every year only has 12 or 14. Pete Rose might get two hundred hits a year. I'd say Rose has a better chance of getting a single with a runner on third than hitting a sacrifice fly. I usually prefer to take three shots with a runner on second with no outs than two shots with a runner on third with one out.

You can work on bunting forever, but if the pitcher surprises the hitter, bunting is tough. Since a manager should only have those hitters bunt who have the skill, about 80 percent of your sacrifices should be successful. That percentage will be much lower if you have a player with marginal bunting ability trying to move a runner along. Usually that's asking for trouble, and you end up either giving up an out without advantage to the runner or giving the pitcher two free strikes on your hitter. Often I wonder if that 80 percent success rate makes the play worth it. With a hitter like Belanger, it's the right move. But with some better hitters, I usually like to let them swing.

The Base on Balls, or Why I Played Glenn Gulliver

There is a lot to be said for the base on balls. It isn't as good as a hit, especially when that hit is a double or a homer, but there are certain guys who can mean a lot to your offense because they draw walks.

Let's start with Tommy Shopay. Tommy was a good player, even if his major-league stats don't show it. Look at what he did when he went back to Class AAA: he tore up the International League, outhitting some guys who later became stars in the big leagues. But Tommy was in an unfortunate situation with us. He was an outfielder in the early 1970s when we had guys like Don Buford, Paul Blair, Frank Robinson, Don Baylor, Al Bumbry, Ken Singleton, and Merv Rettenmund. It wasn't his fault that he didn't get in the lineup, nor was it my fault for not playing him. It was just circumstances. He was a good player, but we had better players in front of him. Tom would hit .340 or .350 in the minors, and there isn't *that* big a difference between Rochester and Baltimore.

Shopay was a base-on-balls man. His record in the minors showed it. But when he did get into the lineup with Baltimore, he didn't do one of the things he did best: take pitches and draw walks. He got impatient; he wanted to make the most of every opportunity, and as a consequence, he tried too hard and got away from his game. When I put him in there, he'd be trying to get three hits so he could get more playing time. That's all right in theory, but it didn't work for Tommy. He was up there swinging at everything that was close to the plate. The pitcher would start him off with a neck-high fastball. It was a ball, and in the minors, he would have taken it and then he'd be ahead in the count. But with Baltimore he was so anxious that he'd swing at that first pitch and pop it up. So instead of having a one-ball count, he'd be out.

I never could convince Tommy to take those pitches. I'd play him against Nolan Ryan, because I figured he could draw a walk and start a rally, assuming he wouldn't swing at all those pitches Ryan would throw out of the strike zone. But Tommy would press and keep swinging at those bad pitches.

It sounds like a little thing, but a walk can win a game. For example, a guy leads off an inning with a walk when you're two runs down. That's a big thing, because now you can tie the score with one swing of the bat. That's why I just cringe when I let a guy hit with a 2–0 count and he pops up a pitch that would have been ball three. I love the hitters who can wait for strikes.

As everybody knows, I like the home run. But I like the three-run homer best, and that means there have to be two guys on base when the homer comes. And how did those two guys get on base? Odds are that one of them walked. When I played, I drew a lot of walks. Late in the game, if we needed a walk to get something going, I'd take pitches until there were two strikes on me. Of course, I didn't strike out that much. Also, you don't want your home-run hitters taking too many pitches. But there are some players who can help the club, and themselves, by being more selective at the plate.

It isn't as easy as it sounds. Say a player is hitting .260 and he wants to get that batting average up. Everyone knows that you have to swing to raise your batting average. A walk may start a rally and help the club, but your batting average stays the same. Some players get into a vicious circle. Often a player is hitting lower than he should because he's been swinging at bad pitches or at pitches he can't handle. This is when he should be more careful at the plate, watching the pitches more closely and trying to get ahead in the count. But usually the opposite happens. Since the guy isn't hitting and because he wants to raise his average fast, he's swinging at everything. Consequently, he's making outs on pitches he wouldn't have swung at a month earlier. That .260 batting average soon becomes .230.

The key is patience.

I wish there was a way to convince some players of the importance of walks. Take a guy like Glenn Gulliver. I played him down the stretch in 1982 because of his ability to walk. For a long time he had a batting average in the low .200s, but his on-base percentage was .430. He was helping the club, and there is a place in the majors for a guy like that. I used Gulliver at third because his minor-league record in the Detroit Tigers' system showed he could draw walks. He did it when we had him at our Rochester farm club, and he did it when I had him with the Orioles. At that time I was looking for someone who could get on base in front of Eddie Murray. Murray was batting fourth. Ken Singleton usually has one of the best on-base percentages in the game, and that's why I had him hit third. He does a great job of getting on base, averaging a hundred walks a year since coming to Baltimore. But in 1982 Singleton had an off year. I kept him hitting third most of the time because he had been a productive hitter so often in the past, but I still needed to get someone on base. That was where Gulliver fit in. I batted him second, and he knew his job—draw walks and score runs.

In 1982 Gulliver played in 50 games for me and hit only .200. But the man drew 37 walks. Over the course of the season that would translate to more than a hundred and twenty walks. He was one of the big reasons we were second in the league in walks in 1982.

At the top of the lineup, walks are crucial. Until Don Buford played for me, he didn't appreciate the worth of a walk. I taught him to become one of the best on-base men around, and in our three-straight pennant years of 1969, 1970, and 1971, he averaged 98 walks and 99 runs for me. With his speed and good eye, Buford turned into one of the most dangerous leadoff men around.

We also worked with Al Bumbry, trying to get him to take more pitches and draw more walks. Like a lot of players, he likes to swing at that high pitch. It looks so good, so hittable, but it's out of the strike zone. Also, a player usually hits it straight up, which doesn't do his batting average any good. One of Bumbry's best seasons was 1980, when he hit .318. That year he also had 78 walks, a career high for him.

Don't misunderstand; I'm not saying that a player should go to the plate with the bat glued to his shoulder. Rather, I'm saying that a guy should lay off the bad pitches. It sounds so simple, but it's not. A player who can do it, somebody like Gulliver or Buford, gives you another dimension.

Stolen Bases

In theory, the stolen base is a good weapon, but everything depends on how often it works. For the steal to be worthwhile, the runner should be safe around 75 percent of the time. The player who steals thirty-five bases but is thrown out twenty-five times isn't helping the team. If I had a runner stealing thirty-five bases out of 60 attempts, I'd stop giving him the steal sign. The failed stolen base can be destructive, particularly at the top of the order, because it takes a runner off the basepaths ahead of your home-run hitters.

Some situations in baseball call for a steal. If your leadoff hitter is Rickey Henderson and he starts off an inning by getting on base, let him steal if the score is close. But if you've got a runner on first with two outs and your hitter is someone like Eddie Murray or Jim Rice, keep that runner on first. Forget the stolen base. Rice and Murray might hit the ball out of the park and give you two runs. Power hitters like them also hit a lot of doubles, which will drive in a run from first base, especially when the runner is fast enough to want to steal. If Murray is at the plate with a runner on first, you cannot win by trying to steal. First, the runner might be thrown out, killing the rally. But even if the runner is successful, you've opened up first base, and the pitcher can now pitch around Murray; the steal literally takes the bat out of his hands. I want Murray to swing at every possible opportunity; it's guys like him that win games.

I remember a game in 1976 when Reggie Jackson was playing for the Orioles. Reggie had pretty good speed and he could steal a base. In this instance, Reggie was on first with two outs. A left-hander was pitching to Lee May. May hit a lot of home runs off lefties in his career, but Reggie decided to steal second. He made it, and he thought he made a good play, but the pitcher promptly walked May. I had wanted Lee to have a chance at winning the game in that spot, but the stolen base cost him the opportunity.

I had a sign for my players that allowed them to steal on any pitch on which they felt they had the jump. In other words, they got to pick their own spot. But in some situations, I took that sign off no matter who was on first, because I wanted the hitter to be able to swing the bat. I don't believe in letting the runners steal any time they want.

Some of my players might have stolen more bases for other clubs. Al Bumbry was a fast runner, and I usually let him run if he felt he had the jump, but Al would have stolen an extra ten or fifteen bases a year if he had been with a different team when he was in his prime. Of course, he might not have been on as many pennant winners.

The stolen base, like the bunt, is a play for one run. It improves your chances to score the runner who's on base, but it can make it harder on the hitter. With first base open, the pitcher can pitch around the batter. And that stolen base also makes it tougher to hit a ball through the right side of the infield, since the first baseman doesn't have to hold the runner on anymore. It could take away your chance to get those three or four hits in a row that get you a couple of runs instead of just that single run.

WEAVER'S SIXTH LAW

Don't play for one run unless you know that run will win a ballgame.

Speed is a tremendous asset to a team if you aren't giving up any other part of the game. The stolen base is very important in the eighth or ninth inning. Frank Robinson would steal between ten and fifteen bases a year and be thrown out only once in those crucial situations. That is when a stolen base can be the difference between winning and losing.

I liked to have speed in the lineup so long as I didn't have to sacrifice something else—namely, power, which is what really wins a lot of games. It's very hard to find a player who can hit thirty homers *and* steal bases. Given a choice, I'll take the twenty-five-to-thirty-home-run-a-year player every time.

A team should be built with power hitters first; players with

speed can be added around them. I believe in getting as many
players as possible who can hit the ball out of the park. They are
the hardest to find.

In 1973, we went 97–65, and we won the American League
East. That was a club based on speed, with Al Bumbry, Rich
Coggins, Bobby Grich, Merv Rettenmund, Don Baylor, Paul Blair,
Mark Belanger, and Tommy Davis all stealing at least ten bases
each. We stole a team-record 140 bases and were thrown out 64
times. I gave the steal sign whenever there was the opportunity.
We had 52 bunt hits that year. Earl Williams led us with 22 homers,
followed by Grich, with only 12. The team had only 119 homers. I
prefer my clubs to hit at least 150 homers.

I don't want to take anything away from that club, but it won
the fewest games of any division-winning team I managed. Every
game was a struggle because of our lack of power, our inability to
break it wide open with one swing of the bat. I've managed and
won with guys who hit singles and stole bases, but I'd much rather
have a power club. Those home runs make life a lot easier.

The Hit-and-Run

I don't have a hit-and-run sign, and I believe it's the worst play
in baseball. First, the runner is going to second base at half speed,
looking to see if the hitter makes contact. If the hitter fails to
connect, 90 percent of the time that runner is thrown out stealing
second. Also, the hitter is at a disadvantage because he knows he
has to swing at any pitch in order to protect the runner. Odds are
that he'll be going after a pitch that isn't a particularly good one to
hit. It puts everyone at a disadvantage, and I don't think much of
it.

Now I do have something I call the *run-and-hit*. That is far
different from the standard hit-and-run. With this play, the runner
on first is going full-speed to second. He wants to steal the base
and isn't counting on the hitter to protect him by making contact.
The batter swings at the pitch only if he likes it; he can take it if
it's out of the strike zone. He doesn't have to worry about going
after a poor pitch, because he knows the runner is going all-out to
steal a base. As with the hit-and-run, the right side of the infield
should open up for a right-handed batter when the runner on first

attempts to steal second, since the second baseman must cover the bag to take the throw from the catcher. Rich Dauer and Mark Belanger were great at slapping the ball through the spot vacated by the second baseman. But on the run-and-hit the batter isn't forced to do this. He can take the pitch, or if he gets a pitch he can pull, he's free to swing for the fences.

The runner isn't at a disadvantage, either. When you call the hit-and-run, he must break for second on that pitch no matter what, and often he's running without a decent jump. Under ordinary circumstances there would be no way in hell he'd steal second, but with the play on he must. With the run-and-hit, however, the runner breaks for second only if he has the jump. If he fails to get a decent lead, he stays put.

I used to be a pretty good hit-and-run man when I played in the minors. I handled the bat well and could hit the ball to the right side of the infield. Nevertheless, I know that you often give the opposition an out on the hit-and-run play. That's because you can't trust the pitcher to throw a strike, so the hitter is often waving weakly at a ball that's off the plate. That usually results in a weak grounder that gets the runner to second, but the hitter is easily retired at first. Hell, you may as well bunt! Over the course of the season, only a few guys actually get hits on the hit-and-run play, because everything must go right for it to work. About the only thing you can say for the hit-and-run is that it prevents the double-play grounder. But when you add up the caught stealings, the weak grounders, and the line-drive double-plays, that advantage vanishes. I'll take my chances with a normal swing anytime.

The Squeeze Play

The squeeze play is the most dangerous play in baseball. It can win or lose a game for you right then and there. I used it only about once a year, and that had to be with a good bunter like Belanger. The runner breaks from third base to the plate and the bunter squares around—but the pitcher can mess up the play by throwing a pitch that isn't buntable. The hitter can maybe throw his bat at the pitch, but the best he can do is foul it off.

There is no way to defend against a squeeze bunt. The play requires everything to work perfectly. There is no margin for error.

As the pitcher winds up and throws to home plate, the runner breaks from third base. The batter's job is simply to bunt the ball on the ground.

However, if the runner leaves third base too early, the pitcher may have time to see him and can then throw the ball where the hitter is unable to bunt it. If there's a right-handed hitter at the plate, that pitch would be inside, almost at the batter's head, to make sure he got out of the way. If it's a left-handed hitter, the pitch would be way outside, so that the catcher could receive the ball where the third-base line and plate come together, which puts him in great position to tag out the runner.

The play fails when the runner breaks too early or when the runner or hitter misses the sign. It will also fail when the bunter doesn't make contact or doesn't bunt the ball in fair territory on the ground.

However, if the runner waits until the pitcher releases the ball and then breaks for the plate, and if the hitter bunts the ball on the ground between the foul lines, the play will work no matter what the defense does. If everyone on the offense executes his job properly, it is not physically possible for the defense to get the ball and relay it to home plate in time to catch the runner. But that's an awful lot to ask for. I'd just as soon count on a base hit or sacrifice fly to get the man home.

The First-and-Third Double Steal

This is a pet play of the Baltimore Orioles. We practiced it every spring on our "little infield" down the left-field line in Miami Stadium. We may have used it only once or twice a year, but it won some games for us.

I only used this double-steal play with two outs. There must be runners on first and third. Until there are two outs, I believe the odds are better in letting the hitter attempt to drive in the run from third. This play is designed for when you need one run. If it fails, you come out of the inning with nothing, so it should be employed only in close games.

I usually used this play in extra innings. I wouldn't even go to it in the eighth inning unless my team was in front by two and I wanted another insurance run. It's a very dangerous play.

It's a timing play, and if the pitcher does his job, there is no way it can work. But pitchers often fall into a predictable rhythm late in a game. They may look to the runner at first, then check the runner at third, look back to first, and then throw to the plate. Some guys use this pattern or a variation of it almost all the time with runners on first and third. The manager has to sit on the bench and time it so he can tell his runner at first when to move.

The key is to make sure the pitcher makes a play on the runner at first. Most of the time we used it with a left-handed pitcher on the mound, since from the stretch position he is staring at the runner on first and needs to look over his shoulder to spot the runner at third.

Here is how it works:

1. The team must detect the pattern of the pitcher. How many times does he look to first and third before throwing to the plate? If he does the same thing over and over again, this information is relayed to the runner at first.
2. After the pitcher has completed checking the runners, the man at first base takes a big enough lead to be picked off.
3. The runner on third base breaks for home plate the second the pitcher takes his eye away from third. This means the runner on third is moving *before* the throw to first.
4. If the pitcher throws to first, it is impossible for the runner going home to be caught. His jump is too great. And he's sure to cross the plate before the runner on first is tagged out.

Here is a variation to be used for a right-handed pitcher, who is staring at the runner on third and looking over his shoulder at the runner on first while in the stretch position.

1. Once again, the team must detect the pattern of the pitcher checking the base runners.
2. After the pitcher checks the runners, the runner on first takes a big enough lead to draw a throw. This can also cause the pitcher to balk if he starts to throw to first and then hears someone yell to throw home to nab the runner breaking from third.

3. If the pitcher throws to first, the runner must get into a run-down and draw as many throws as possible, giving the man on third time to get across the plate.

4. In this variation, the runner on first makes the initial move and the runner on third doesn't go until the pitcher begins his move to first base.

In my fifteen years of managing this play probably worked about half the time, but it still is not a good percentage play. You can't use it that often, because there are only certain pitchers you can use it against. Others don't fall into a neat, predictable pattern. At most, it worked twice a year. In the lower levels of baseball, it may work more often, because the players there are more prone to making errors.

THE LINEUP

Pushing the Right
Buttons

THE MOST IMPORTANT JOB a manager does each day is fill out his lineup card. Once the players are in the game, it's up to them to produce; all a manager can do is put the best team on the field. I took several things into consideration in making out a lineup.

The leadoff hitter should be someone with a high on-base percentage, a guy who draws seventy or more walks and hits for a high average. When Al Bumbry was hitting .317, he was ideal. The first inning is the only time a manager is given the chance to set up the batting order exactly the way he wants it. After that it's rare for the leadoff hitter to start an inning. My goal is to have as many players on base as possible when the number-four hitter comes to bat. In the first inning you want to get the cleanup man up there with a couple of guys on, so I like to get my best on-base men in the first three spots of the order. For years, I used Ken Singleton in the number-three slot, ahead of Eddie Murray. Singleton was good for a hundred walks a year and an on-base percentage over .400. That brought Murray to bat with at least one runner on, so he had the opportunity to do some serious damage.

Some managers like to have a leadoff hitter who reaches base often and a number-two man who is a good bunter. The thinking is that the number-two hitter will bunt or hit-and-run the leadoff man into scoring position. This is designed to get a quick run. Once in a while, I would use Mark Belanger in the second spot of the order for this purpose. Even though Mark was a low-average hitter, he was a dependable bunter. But I'd only do this if the opposing pitcher was someone Belanger could hit or if our pitcher was hot and likely to make a few runs stand up. As a rule, I don't like to bunt in the early innings, because no one can say how important that first-inning run will be.

The number-five hitter should have some power, be dangerous enough so the opposition can't pitch around your cleanup man. For many years I hit Brooks Robinson sixth. Brooks was prone to hitting into a lot of double plays because he was slow going from home to first base. It wasn't his fault, but it was a fact. Often I batted a fast runner like Paul Blair in front of Brooks. That way, when Blair was on first and Brooks hit a ground ball, Blair's speed would often enable him to get to the man at second making the pivot and break up the double play with a good slide.

A set lineup is fine except for a couple of things—players go into slumps, and they don't hit every pitcher equally well. I move players up and down in the batting order according to how my stats show they have fared against certain pitchers. For the most part, Eddie Murray and Frank Robinson were my cleanup hitters. They handled most pitchers very well. But a player like Gary Roenicke might bat fifth against one pitcher, seventh against another, and not be in the lineup at all against a third. It all depends on the numbers. I believe the lineup has to be changed because of slumps and stats.

Ideally, a manager wants nine players who can run and hit the ball out, but that never happens, so you have to adjust.

Vital Statistics

From the day I took over the Orioles I wanted all the statistical information I could get. Maybe I wouldn't use everything, but I wanted to see it. I believe that what you don't know can hurt you and that you can never know enough. We had charts that showed how our hitters did against every pitcher in the league. It's the most important information you can have. Its worth is impossible to measure, but you'd better believe the charts helped us win a lot of games.

On the day of a game the first thing I did when I arrived at the park was to examine the sheet showing how our hitters performed against that night's starting pitcher.

The accompanying charts show how our hitters did against two pitchers: Lary Sorensen, a pitcher we hit fairly well, and Larry Gura, a lefty who gave us a difficult time.

I'll start with Sorensen.

By examining the chart, you can see that several of our hitters were very successful against him. Nine hitters hit .300 or better against him. When I saw numbers like those, I usually felt confident going into the game. I didn't know that we would hit Sorensen on that particular day, but I knew we had done well against him before.

Ken Singleton had a .667 batting average against Sorensen, so you can be sure I'd want Kenny in the lineup. The same holds true for Al Bumbry (.450), Eddie Murray (.333), Rich Dauer (.333), Cal Ripken (.500), and John Lowenstein (.333).

Assuming those players were healthy and not in a severe slump, right away I'd have Lowenstein in left, Bumbry in center, Singleton in right, Murray at first, Dauer at second, and Ripken at short. The open spots would be designated hitter, third base, and catcher.

Behind the plate, my choices were Rick Dempsey and Joe Nolan. Dempsey had some problems with Sorensen (three for twenty-five), while Nolan was a .333 hitter. I usually would go with Nolan in a situation like this.

DH possibilities were Terry Crowley (.400), Benny Ayala (.000), Dan Ford (.143), and Gary Roenicke (.167). Crowley would be the clear-cut choice. Of the four, he was the only left-handed hitter, and did a good job hitting off-speed pitches. Sorensen is a right-hander who throws a lot of sinkers and changeups. The only way I might *not* use Crowley would be if Ford was swinging a very hot bat. Even though Ford had some problems with Sorensen, I might play him if he was hitting everybody in sight and keep Crowley on the bench and ready in case I needed a pinch hitter.

At third base, I'd have Leo Hernandez or Lenn Sakata. Be-

PITCHER: Lary Sorensen   RHP   4–5   5.87 ERA vs. Baltimore

Name	AB	H	2B	3B	HR	RBI	BA
Al Bumbry	20	9	2	1	0	7	.450
Ken Singleton	24	16	5	2	3	12	.667
Rick Dempsey	25	3	0	0	0	1	.120
Terry Crowley	10	4	1	0	1	4	.400
Benny Ayala	2	0	0	0	0	0	.000
Joe Nolan	9	3	1	0	0	2	.333
Eddie Murray	30	10	2	0	2	7	.333
Rich Dauer	18	6	0	0	0	3	.333
Cal Ripken	6	3	1	0	1	3	.500
John Lowenstein	15	5	1	0	1	4	.333
Gary Roenicke	12	2	1	0	0	0	.167
Dan Ford	21	3	0	0	0	1	.143
Leo Hernandez	3	0	0	0	0	0	.000
Lenn Sakata	2	1	0	0	0	0	.500

PITCHER: Larry Gura   LHP   10–5   2.70 ERA vs. Baltimore

Name	AB	H	2B	3B	HR	RBI	BA
Al Bumbry	20	4	0	0	0	1	.200
Ken Singleton	28	7	1	0	2	6	.250
Rick Dempsey	30	5	0	0	1	2	.167
Terry Crowley	2	0	0	0	0	0	.000
Benny Ayala	12	4	1	0	1	4	.333
Joe Nolan	4	1	0	0	0	0	.250
Eddie Murray	35	15	4	1	3	11	.427
Rich Dauer	25	5	1	0	0	3	.200
Cal Ripken	6	1	0	0	0	0	.167
John Lowenstein	3	0	0	0	0	0	.000
Gary Roenicke	18	4	1	0	1	4	.222
Dan Ford	24	4	1	0	2	5	.167
Leo Hernandez	0	0	0	0	0	0	.000
Lenn Sakata	4	0	0	0	0	0	.000

cause Hernandez was a rookie, he had faced Sorensen in only one game. Most of the time, I think a player needs around twenty at bats before I can get a reading on him against a certain pitcher. I would use Leo to give him more time to compile a track record against Sorensen.

It was much tougher to come up with a lineup against Larry Gura. First, Murray and Ayala were the only two .300 hitters against Gura. In fact, they were the only guys hitting over .250. When I saw these numbers, I assumed that we probably wouldn't score a lot of runs in the game. It also meant that I would have to examine the chart closely and figure out who had the best chance of doing something against Gura.

I would probably start with Ayala as the DH and Murray at first. Even though Dauer was a .200 hitter against Gura, he'd be my second baseman: Rich is a dependable glove man, and he had not been overwhelmed by Gura. Because they were young players and the guys I was trying to break in, I'd use Ripken at short and Hernandez at third.

Behind the plate, I would use Dempsey, even though he was a .167 hitter against Gura. The major reason would be Rick's arm, not his bat. The Royals have a lot of speed, and they love to steal bases. Dempsey is one of the best throwing catchers in baseball, so I'd play him. Also, Nolan is a left-handed hitter, and Gura usually gives lefty hitters fits.

The outfield would be a complicated situation. Despite the fact that Ford was a .167 hitter against Gura, I'd play Dan, because he had two homers off Gura and three of his four hits had been for extra bases. If he connected, Ford could be productive. So I'd play Ford in left field and Singleton, a .250 hitter off Gura, in right. Like Ford, Singleton had two homers off Gura.

That left center field, with Bumbry and Roenicke being the candidates. I'd probably go with whoever was on a hot streak. If both were playing at their usual levels, I'd go with Roenicke. Both players had four hits, but all of Bumbry's had been singles, while Roenicke had a home run and a double.

One of the most difficult parts of managing is to decide how long you can stick with a player who isn't doing the job. Rich Dauer started off 1977, his rookie season, one for forty-four. He had taken over for Bobby Grich, who had gone to California as a

STEVE STONE, DESIGNATED HITTER

In 1981 I wrote Steve Stone into my lineup every day as the designated hitter. Stone is a pitcher, and I naturally did not expect him to hit. In fact, the first time I did it, Stone wasn't even with the club—he had flown ahead to the next city on the road trip because he was scheduled to pitch the following day. During this season I often platooned Benny Ayala and Terry Crowley as my designated hitters. I usually batted them sixth in the lineup. Let's say the Orioles were playing Cleveland and Len Barker was starting for the Indians. I'd have Terry Crowley in the lineup against the right-handed Barker. But suppose the first five hitters get to Barker and knock him out. The Indians bring in Rick Waits, a lefty. I wouldn't want to use Crowley against Waits, so I would have to bat Ayala for Crowley. But in the process, I've lost Crowley without him making an appearance. That's wasting a player. Or what if a pitcher takes the mound, throws to a couple of hitters, and then leaves because his arm hurts. It may happen only twice a season, but there is no reason to waste a player if it can be avoided.

By listing a pitcher such as Stone as the DH, I have the option of sending up Crowley *or* Ayala. I don't lose a player. But baseball didn't like this idea, and they passed a rule against it. The establishment said it was playing hell with the pinch-hit statistics, because that first at bat every game for the DH was then considered a pinch-hit appearance. But it wasn't against the rules. No one was outsmarting anyone. Once the idea became a reality, anyone could do it. The only reason they stopped me from using a pitcher as the DH was for the integrity of statistics. That's a pretty weak reason, if you ask me.

free agent. In 1976 Rich had led the International League in hitting, batting .336 at Rochester. Early in the 1977 season it was the only thing he had going for him. The scouting reports on Dauer were very good. Yet he was batting one for forty-four and killing us offensively. I knew that one for forty-four could not be the true Rich Dauer. I was counting on it, because I kept writing his name in the lineup. Someone has to give a rookie a chance. I knew he could not be that bad a hitter—one for forty-four is an .023 batting average. I found it hard to believe that the International League batting champ could go out and be one for forty-four. That's unthinkable.

I had Rich in and out of the lineup. Billy Smith was playing some second base, too, and Smith was playing well, hitting the ball hard. It was difficult to take Smith out of there because he produced, but I wanted to get Dauer established. This wasn't a special favor; rather, I believed Dauer would ultimately be the better player and should be given a legitimate opportunity.

The worst part about that first year was when I called Dauer into my office. I said, "Rich, you're not hitting. What's wrong?" He said nothing was wrong. But I said, "There must be something wrong. You're one for forty-four and losing ballgames." He sort of shrugged.

At that time the pitching was a little beyond Rich. He was waiting for the pitchers to make mistakes, but pitchers don't foul up as often in the majors as they do in the International League. He was swinging at far more pitches than he took.

When I managed, I didn't break rookies in, they broke themselves in. But I used them so they wouldn't be run out of the league. Take a young left-handed hitter. It isn't wise to keep him in the lineup against all left-handed pitchers, because the veterans will probably give him a hard time. If a manager doesn't have patience, too many lefties could chase the rookie out of the league. The manager has to have patience and use the rookie with discretion: use him against a few lefties and ease him into the majors while keeping his batting average respectable.

I like to use players so they don't have to go back to the minors. That means there may be some rocky times, as when Dauer was one for forty-four or when Mike Flanagan was 2–8 or when Cal Ripken was hitting around .100 early in his rookie year. The manager uses the players so they can help him win a few games but doesn't use them when they would be outclassed to the point that they have to be farmed out.

Ballplayers probably don't appreciate this, because they don't like being out of the lineup, whether they're a rookie or a veteran. They all want to play every day. But I don't care if the guy is in his fourth year, his first year, or his fifteenth year. The manager knows it's for the best of the club when he puts a player on the bench. No manager will put a player in the lineup when he thinks he'll lose with him, just as no manager will keep a player on the bench if he believes that player can win that particular game.

If you're facing a pitcher who gives your team fits, you must make some moves. A manager may look at his stats and see that no one really hits this pitcher. Why not try some players who have no stats against him? Maybe those batters will get some hits. It's up to a manager to keep searching for a combination that works.

I have nothing against being called a push-button manager. Early in my career it might have bothered me. But think about it. What else does a manager do but push buttons? He doesn't hit, he doesn't run, he doesn't throw, and he doesn't catch the ball. A manager has twenty-five players, or twenty-five buttons, and he selects which one he'll use, or push, that day. The manager who presses the right buttons most often is the one who wins the most games. When a manager has been pushing the same buttons day after day and losing, he'd better start pushing some different ones. The key to managing is player evaluation, which is another way of saying that you must know which buttons to push and when to push them.

The left-field platoon the Orioles had in 1982 developed because we didn't have one player who I felt could do the job out there every day. So I used John Lowenstein, Benny Ayala, and Gary Roenicke. A left-handed hitter, Lowenstein was going to hit some righties better than Roenicke. Roenicke or Ayala could hit all lefties better than Lowenstein. So you follow your stats and maybe consider who is swinging the hot bat. Most of all, you attempt to get the best player in left field for that particular day.

There is no way to know why some hitters don't hit some pitchers, but it's an undeniable fact. Sometimes a player will have trouble with a pitcher early in his career and then hit him later on, but usually the statistics are pretty consistent. Rich Dauer has learned to hit some pitchers who made his life miserable early in his career. That's probably a matter of Dauer remembering what those pitchers were doing when they got him out and then adjusting to it. At the same time the pitchers haven't changed their approach to Dauer. Hitters and pitchers should make adjustments all the time.

Boog Powell was two for sixty-one against Mickey Lolich. That is something that never changed, and it never was going to change. Boog Powell was not going to hit Mickey Lolich. Period. Mark Belanger hit well over .300 against Jim Kern and Nolan Ryan, but he was barely a .200 hitter against the rest of the league.

Another unbelievable statistic was that Pat Kelly was six for eight against Detroit's Dave Rozema—with four of those hits being home runs. If Rozema was in the game, I'd do everything in my power to get Kelly up to bat. With overwhelming numbers like those, you have to get Kelly up there. Conversely, if I were the opposing manager, I wouldn't want Rozema pitching to Kelly. That's common sense.

In my early years with the Orioles Curt Motton was three for five off Rudy May. The three hits were home runs. Not bad for a guy who had only 25 major league homers!

Many of the players know how they fare against each other. Jim Palmer has a great memory and he can recall many games almost pitch by pitch; he doesn't need cards to know how a certain hitter has fared against him. During a game he would remind people that this guy had handled him pretty well. Two of the players who gave Palmer fits were Craig Reynolds and Doug Griffin. Palmer would say late in a game, "Griffin is coming up, and don't let me get in trouble. Griffin is hitting about .400 against me." That's what makes baseball so damn interesting. Griffin was a lifetime .245 hitter, but he batted .400 against a great like Palmer.

In theory a batter should have twenty at bats against a pitcher before you can get a true reading on how he will do. But in the case of Kelly versus Rozema or Motton versus May, a handful of at bats was enough. If I have a hitter who is four for nine against a certain pitcher, that's a pretty good indication to me that I should play the guy. The gray area is when a hitter is two for eight or three for twelve with no homers. That doesn't tell you much. The hitter is not helpless against the pitcher, but he hasn't had a field day, either. Basically you need more at bats to tell.

You can't manage strictly by stats. They just give you something else to go on. As I have said countless times, a manager and a player should be willing to consider all the information available. They don't always have to follow it, but they should pay some attention to it. There is nothing like finding out a little extra—it can be the difference between winning and losing a game.

If you know that Ken Singleton is eight for fifteen against Larry Sorensen, it can help win a game. It's better than going up against Sorensen and not having any statistics.

THE LEFT-HANDED SHORTSTOP

This is something I did in September of 1975. Mark Belanger was a .220 hitter for me during most of his career, but he was also the greatest defensive shortstop I have ever seen. I spent some time trying to figure out how I could get the best of both worlds—a good bat and Belanger's amazing glove. I came up with this plan, which is still legal.

When my team was on the road, I would list someone else as our leadoff hitter and shortstop. Often it was Royle Stillman, a young out-fielder we had brought up from Rochester. Stillman would bat in the top of the first, and then Belanger would go in to play shortstop in the bottom of the inning. For the rest of the game, Belanger was the leadoff hitter and shortstop. But I did manage to get that one at bat from an effective hitter. What's more, Stillman was four for nine in those games. That's .444, which isn't too bad. His on-base percentage was over .500. We also did it in 1979, with Tom Chism, a first baseman.

I used this strategy only in September, when the roster swelled from twenty-five to forty and we had plenty of players available. During the regular season, before September 1, I was reluctant to use it, because I didn't want to use up a player in the top of the first inning: I might need him later to go to the plate and win the game. But in September it's a no-risk situation.

Usually Mark Belanger was the one who suffered. It hurt him to lose that at bat. Oh, he just hated it. In those moments, Mark was too upset to think what was best for the team. That's a very human reaction, but the manager is only seeking to do whatever he can to win the game. It was nothing personal against Mark or anyone else. What the hell, Stillman went four for nine and got on base half the time. It's hard to argue with those results.

Strict right-left platooning has been a part of baseball for a long time, although Casey Stengel was the first to make it known when he managed the Yankees in the 1950s. He platooned Gene Woodling and Hank Bauer in the outfield. Woodling was a left-handed hitter, and Bauer swung from the right side. Bauer was going to hit left-handers better than Woodling, and Woodling was going to hit some right-handers better than Bauer. It doesn't always work out, but the percentages are with you. It generally is easier to hit a ball breaking toward you than away from you.

A team strives to have nine players to put out there every day who can do everything. Then you don't have to worry about platooning or juggling. The 1982 California Angels won the American League West because they had four former M.V.P.'s in their lineup. It's hard to go wrong when you write Rod Carew, Don Baylor, Reggie Jackson, and Fred Lynn into the lineup every day. In four different years, those players did more than anyone else in the league. If you have the four of them on one team and then can fill in around them with Bobby Grich, Tim Foli, Bob Boone, Brian Downing, and Doug DeCinces, you have one hell of a team.

While some teams didn't have a high opinion of some of our players, like Benny Ayala, Pat Kelly, Curt Motton, and John Lowenstein, they were distinguished players to me. They were better than many players I saw on other teams. When Pat Kelly and John Lowenstein played against the Orioles, they hurt us. I was impressed by what I saw, and I thought it would be great if the Orioles could obtain them. I figured that if these players had the ability to hurt my team, they could do a lot for me.

Some people have been impressed by the Yankee bench of recent years, with Oscar Gamble, Lou Piniella, Bobby Murcer, and others. These guys were making a lot of money and had talent, but salary has nothing to do with it when that batter goes to home plate. I like those Yankee hitters, but my bench was just as productive. Maybe they didn't make as much as the Yankee reserves, but that's not the point. As I said before, it all comes down to getting the right hitter at bat at the right time.

No matter how convincing the stats are, no platoon arrangement's going to work if the players can't accept their roles. A player needs the proper attitude to be effective coming off the bench. If a player keeps saying, "I never did this before, I always was a regular, there's no way I can sit and hit," then he won't hit. He's talked himself out of it. Or if the player constantly complains about not starting, it's doubtful that he'll be any good coming off the bench. Once a player says, "Coming off the bench is my job; if the manager calls on me, I'm going to be ready to contribute," then he'll probably do just that. John Lowenstein looks at the situation this way. That is why he is dynamite in his role. He doesn't gripe, his mind is on the game, and he is prepared when the call comes.

Some guys have a difficult time adjusting to the bench. Terry Crowley was one. In his rookie year with Baltimore, 1970, he batted 152 times, hitting .257 with five homers. That was a decent season. But Boog Powell was our first baseman in 1970, and Crowley was not as good as Boog. It was that simple, and that doesn't take anything away from Crowley, because Boog was a superb player. Platooning wasn't even a possibility, because both Terry and Boog were left-handed hitters. But that wasn't enough for Terry. He wanted a chance to make his mark. He also wanted to make some money, and he wasn't going to make a lot sitting on the bench, especially in 1970, which was before big salaries became a part of the game. Terry overrated his talent. He had pretty good talent, but his overall game was not as good as he believed. He asked to be traded. The front office said that when they found someone who could replace him, they would swap him, and in 1974 Crowley was sold to Texas. He didn't make the team in spring training, and the Rangers sold him to Cincinnati. The Reds' manager in 1974 was Sparky Anderson, and he saw that Terry would make a good left-handed pinch hitter. Sparky told Crowley what he had in mind, in almost the same words I had said to Terry many times over the years. Basically, Terry was a part-time player. At that point of Crowley's career, he accepted that role with the Reds. He even said, "At least they tell me what I have to do over here." Of course, I had told him that before, but he wasn't ready to believe it.

Hitting ability doesn't diminish. A good hitter usually stays good for a long time. Terry spent two years with the Reds, batting 125 times in 1974 and 71 times in 1975, which was less playing time than he had had in three full seasons under me when he was complaining about sitting on the bench.

Before the 1976 season Cincinnati sold Terry to Atlanta. The Reds probably had found someone who could pinch-hit as well as Terry and maybe pinch-run, too, which was a skill Terry lacked.

When it comes to forming a bench, a team is always looking for a player with as many skills as possible. If a guy can pinch-hit *and* pinch-run, he immediately becomes more valuable than a player who can only pinch-hit. So Terry went to the Braves, but they released him in spring training. After he was cut, Terry called us. We didn't have any room for him on the big-league roster: in 1976 I had Lee May and Tony Muser for first base. But we knew that Terry was still a pretty good hitter, so we signed him to a Rochester contract. Crowley went to Rochester and did pretty well, and we called him up at the end of the year. In 1977 Terry went back to Rochester and ripped up the International League, hitting .308 with 30 homers in 108 games. We called him up in September, and he hit .364 coming off the bench. He stayed with the Orioles after that, content to do the job as a left-handed pinch hitter, with maybe some spot duty at first. He had matured and did the job he couldn't handle as a rookie.

In the past, I have had some good hitters on the bench—Jose Morales, Lowenstein, Ayala, Kelly, and Crowley. Some may believe we didn't have enough versatility on the bench, that we were overloaded with bats. But we kept winning, and those guys kept supplying big hits.

Jim Northrup is another guy who did a nice job for me. We had him in 1975, when he was thirty-five. He was an experienced player who could still hit. Jim had lost a little defensively, but I still used him to fill in as a center fielder. In 1974, Northrup hit .571 for us in eight games down the stretch, and hit .357 in the 1974 American League playoffs for us. Jim was a big reason we won the American League East. He had been around and he was intelligent, and those guys are a pleasure to have on the bench.

On my bench I emphasized hitting, because the bench guys are around for offense. Often they're not as good defensively as the regulars. What they will do is step into the lineup if some of your nine guys on the field aren't producing offensively.

The players who are your regulars are more than likely pretty good defensive ballplayers. But there are times in the season when a team gets into a rut of losing 1–0, 2–1, and 3–2. That's when a manager has to get some punch into the lineup. It's bad for morale when the pitchers begin thinking they have to throw a shutout every time they take the mound.

When we weren't hitting and weren't winning, Mark Belanger was the first guy to come out. As great as Mark was on defense, there were periods in the year when we had to get another bat in the lineup. If you don't get runs, you can't win.

Some players can work their way into a starting role. Take Curt Motton and Al Bumbry. Motton was strictly an offensive player. Why he didn't improve his defense was a matter of attitude. He was happy to be in the majors, but he didn't like working on defense and didn't spend much time on it. Bumbry also came to the majors as a mediocre left fielder. But Bumbry wasn't content with his defense. He worked and worked, taking thousands of fungoes from the coaches, practicing his defense by catching balls hit during batting practice. He worked out in all three outfield positions and learned to play well enough so that he became a regular center fielder.

No player likes to be lifted for a pinch hitter. I never heard of a player who wanted to be pinch-hit for. That goes against human nature. The player is bound to be angry if you pinch-hit for him. But in most of these instances, it's twenty-four against one. Forget the manager and forget the coaching staff. Just consider the other players. When I let a player bat in the eighth inning of a close game and I know he should be called back for a pinch hitter, there are twenty-four players who know the exact same thing. If a manager doesn't make the move because he doesn't want to hurt the feelings of one player, he loses the respect of the other twenty-four.

A manager can attempt to rationalize the situation by saying, "Well, the player has to hit sometime," or "I'm trying to build his confidence." But if the manager sends the guy up to the plate when he is pretty much overmatched and he strikes out, that takes care of his confidence right there. Not only did the manager fail to make the proper move, but the player is worse off for it. He knows he let the other twenty-four players down. Believe me, he feels it in his gut, and he knows it in his head. After it's over, the player might even ask himself why the manager let him go up to the plate and strike out, when someone like Terry Crowley could have gone up there and won the game.

Managers may miss some pinch-hitting moves by accident or by looking at the situation differently from the players. Often there are factors that come into question that players can't understand because they aren't thinking along the same lines as the manager. However, to let a player go up there who has whiffed his first three times or has looked terrible at the plate all game is ridiculous. Say it's the eighth inning of a close game and the bases are loaded with one out. Rick Dempsey is hitting for the Orioles against Fergie Jenkins. Dempsey has a batting average just barely over .100 against Jenkins, and Fergie's slider gives Rick all sorts of trouble. If a manager has Terry Crowley sitting on the bench and doesn't use him to hit for Dempsey, there's something wrong. The manager has to make the move and not worry about Dempsey throwing his bat because he won't be given a chance to win the ballgame. Furthermore, as I have said before, the other twenty-four players know you have to go to Crowley. Most of the time the players know what should be done.

PITCHING

The Game Within
the Game

WHEN people ask me to simplify my approach to baseball, I often reply that the way to win is with pitching and three-run homers. While everyone knows how much I love the home run, notice that I mention the word *pitching* first. Pitching is the most important part of the game.

While I was managing the Orioles, they had at least one twenty-game winner for thirteen straight years, which is a major-league record. Nine different pitchers combined for twenty-two twenty-game seasons. In 1971 four Oriole pitchers—Dave McNally, Mike Cuellar, Jim Palmer, and Pat Dobson—won twenty games. That was only the second time in baseball history that four pitchers on one team had won twenty games in the same season. The Orioles also captured six Cy Young Awards while I was manager.

I'm proud of all the twenty-game winners I had with Baltimore, and no matter what people say, I was a part of it. I had a say in acquiring them from other teams and in giving them information about hitters. It comes down to recognizing ability, and that has always been my strong suit. Of course, we also put together good teams with the Orioles. That will help a pitcher win the extra two or three games that he might not with another team.

Over the years, I've gone with a four-man rotation more often than any other manager. This gives the pitchers chances for more wins. It means more starts for each pitcher. I look at it this way: if you have four pitchers who are winning for you and you can get them to the mound more often, it means more wins for the team. The starts you give to your fifth-best starter are taken away from the four who are better than him. Most teams prefer a five-man rotation, but there is nothing wrong with a four-man rotation. Physically, the Orioles have proved that pitchers can last in a four-man rotation. There are some pitchers who can't, but most guys handle it well. Winning twenty games comes from pitchers working between 250 and 300 innings a year. Look at Gaylord Perry and Jim Palmer; those guys won a lot of games in a four-man rotation, pitching over 250 innings a season. They did it year after year.

Fergie Jenkins is another example. He has that longevity and a great success rate, and he did it in a four-man rotation. For the most part, I subscribe to a four-man rotation. Now, Oriole lefty Mike Flanagan threw a little harder when he was in a five-man rotation—that extra day of rest between starts helped him. But Flanagan still had enough stuff to win every fourth day. In the last ten years, most teams have gone with five starters, and I don't know why. I used my fifth starter to pitch in doubleheaders and when I wanted to slightly alter my rotation—for example, when I wanted to keep from starting a lefty in Fenway Park because of the short left-field wall. For that left-hander I might substitute the fifth starter if he was a righty. But all in all I just don't see using a five-man rotation all year for one simple reason:

WEAVER'S SEVENTH LAW

It's easier to find four good starters than five.

Even though I can't throw a curve, I can judge pitchers with my eyes. You start with speed. Does he throw hard enough, or is his fastball sneaky enough to keep the hitters off balance? Is that fastball alive? Does it move on the way to the plate or come in straight and flat?

Warren Spahn used to say that hitting is timing and pitching is upsetting timing. That's why changing speeds on your pitches is so important. The radar gun can be a big help here. It shows a pitcher's speed and also the difference in velocity between his fastball, slider, curve, and changeup. If a guy has an 82-mile-an-hour fastball, a 78-mile-an-hour changeup won't do him any good. That becomes nothing more than a fat fastball. But if a guy has a 90-mile-an-hour fastball and a 78-mile-an-hour change, that will work, because there's a big enough difference. When Mike Flanagan is at his best, his fastball is 89 miles an hour and his change is in the 73-to-75 range. Now that's a wide enough range to throw off a hitter's stride.

When the Orioles got Mike Torrez in 1975, I knew he had a fine fastball and maybe the best slider in the majors. But he had a clear need for a slow curve, something to get the hitters off balance. I mentioned this to George Bamberger, and being the great pitching coach he was, George went right to work with Torrez and taught him that slow curve. It helped to make Torrez a twenty-game winner. In order to be a consistent winner, a pitcher needs some type of slow pitch that he can get over the plate to keep the hitter from sitting on the fastball.

Many people marvel at the success some pitchers have had when they've come to the Orioles. Mike Torrez, Pat Dobson, Mike Cuellar, and Steve Stone had their only twenty-win seasons with Baltimore. Part of that was due to our infield, which made the plays, and to the team in general, which was a winner and scored its share of runs. Obviously, a pitcher will win more games with a better team.

But I believe there is more to it than just a change of scenery. We saw the potential in some of these pitchers, and again, that falls under the heading of baseball judgment.

We recognized that Dobson and Stone had great curveballs. So we wondered why they weren't winning. Maybe they threw their curves too much at some times and not enough at others. Here's where a manager and a pitching coach can help turn a pitcher around. In the second or third inning, the manager might tell the pitcher that his curve isn't worth a damn on this particular day and that maybe he should forget about it for this one game. You don't always have to throw a pitch for it to be a weapon. I remember a game where Tippy Martinez came in from the bullpen and threw three straight fastballs past Cecil Cooper. Cooper never moved his bat, because he was waiting for Tippy's curve, which is his best pitch. An intelligent guy, Cooper was aware of Tippy's curve, overly concerned about it. You can call it "outsmarted" or "outdumbed," but it sure was smart for Tippy. He got Cooper to watch three fastballs.

TWENTY-GAME WINNERS UNDER WEAVER

1968	Dave McNally	22–10	1973	Jim Palmer	22–9
1969	Dave McNally	20–7	1974	Mike Cuellar	22–10
	Mike Cuellar	23–11	1975	Jim Palmer	23–11
1970	Dave McNally	24–9		Mike Torrez	20–9
	Mike Cuellar	24–8	1976	Jim Palmer	22–13
	Jim Palmer	20–10		Wayne Garland	20–7
1971	Dave McNally	21–5	1977	Jim Palmer	20–11
	Mike Cuellar	20–9	1978	Jim Palmer	21–12
	Jim Palmer	20–9	1979	Mike Flanagan	23–9
	Pat Dobson	20–8	1980	Steve Stone	25–7
1972	Jim Palmer	21–10		Scott McGregor	20–8

Sometimes the problem with a pitcher isn't in his pitching. When we traded for Mike Cuellar, we could see from the statistics that he had great ability. In 1967 he was 16–11 with a 3.03 ERA for a Houston team that wasn't very strong. The year before he was 12–10 with a 2.22 ERA for Houston, and that ERA was the second best of any left-hander in the National League, topped only by Sandy Koufax. These are things you have to know. We obtained Mike after the 1968 season, when he went 8–11 with a fine 2.74 ERA.

When I was managing winter ball in Puerto Rico, I had the opportunity to watch Mike throw, and he stood some good big-league hitters right on their ears. I remember seeing him pitch a winter game in which he whiffed Lee May four straight times. Now that tells you something. Lee was a strong right-handed-hitting power man who usually had a field day against left-handers. But he couldn't touch Cuellar, because Cuellar had a devastating screwball. Mike pitched against my team, and I had such hitters as Orlando Cepeda, Tony Perez, Paul Blair, and Dave Johnson. Cuellar made them look silly. So when it came time to make a trade for a guy like Mike, I remembered what he had done in winter ball, what I had seen myself, and then I checked the book. Of course, he would be a great acquisition.

The problem Mike had with Houston was a language problem. A lot of people talked to Mike, and he would just nod at them and say OK, but actually he didn't understand what had been said to him. If a manager started getting excited and talking fast in English, Mike wouldn't be able to understand. Soon, the manager would be going on and on to Mike in English and Mike would be answering in Spanish and no one would have the slightest idea of what was going on. But any time I spoke to Mike, especially in his first few years with the Orioles, I had Elrod Hendricks with me. Elrod was born in the Virgin Islands and spoke both Spanish and English, and it was through him that we established communication with Mike, who was born in Cuba. The words could be said in English and/or Spanish and there would be complete understanding. Mike's first year with us was 1969, and he went 23–11. With him it was a matter of getting to a better club and straightening out the language difficulty.

In his only full season with the Orioles, 1977, Rudy May was 18–14. Rudy was always a good pitcher. He had a fine overhand curve, a big one, but he bounced it in the dirt too much. His curve had to be altered so that he could get it over the plate. Also, there would be nights when May could not control his curve and had to learn to forget the curve and to do something else. It's very basic: if a pitcher is going to lose with his curve, he shouldn't throw it. A pitcher might argue that he can't win without his curve. I'd say, try and win without it; see what happens when you use another pitch. If you get hit using your other pitches, I'll come out of the dugout and get you, we have guys to pitch in relief. But you can't win with the curve tonight.

I realize that some people were surprised that May, Dobson, Stone, Torrez, and Cuellar came into their own after they had been in the majors quite a while. They were no longer kids when we got them. But every pitcher wants to win and make more money. If a manager can have a little success early when a pitcher takes his suggestions, it makes it easier the next time he has something to say. Let's go back to that pitcher who's having a bad night with his curve. Suppose he took the manager's advice, put the curve on the shelf for a night and managed to come away with a win. He will be far more open to advice the next time the manager has something to say. And, of course, these men were smart enough to realize that our four-man rotation gave them a good shot at twenty wins, which could mean more money for them.

There were several reasons for Steve Stone's finding himself with Baltimore. For one, he was supported by an infield that was much better than the one he had behind him when he was with the White Sox. That made two important differences. First, since a curveball pitcher like Stone gives up so many ground balls, the strong Oriole infield made his curve more valuable. Second, the strong infield built up his confidence, and confidence is a necessary ingredient of a winner. Like Rudy May, Stone had a great curve. Naturally, he got into a groove with that curve, and he could throw it over the plate and to the spot he wanted. But until he came to Baltimore, I don't believe Stone was willing to throw his fastball high in the strike zone. He didn't have confidence in his high fastball, and maybe that came from the days when he pitched for the Cubs in Wrigley Field. There, if you throw a high fastball and the batter hits a fly ball, it can get up in the wind and go for a home run. In other parks it's just a harmless fly ball.

What a manager did when he was a player is sometimes relevant to the way he views pitchers. When I played, I had trouble with the high fastball. Like most guys, I was a low-ball hitter, and the smart pitchers would throw me one fastball after another up around my shoulders.

I believe more hitters can be pitched high than low. I've always felt that most hitters are low-ball hitters. Scott McGregor struck out Reggie Jackson four times in a game on high fastballs. Off low pitches, the batter usually hits a line drive or a ground ball. On a high pitch the batter often pops up. Of course, some homers come off high pitches. That's why a high fastball must have something on it and be either inside or outside. A high fastball about 80 miles an hour down the heart of the plate is a batting-practice pitch. But I'm always surprised that more pitchers don't use the high fastball in the American League.

Sometimes you have to let a pitcher make a mistake in order to get your point across. That was the case with Steve Stone. It's not screaming in the beginning, but giving him the information. When the pitcher won't listen, you let him get beat. After it happens, you sit the pitcher down and ask if he wants to be a loser all his life. I had to say to Stone, "You're a loser. You were a loser before you got here. If you want to shut your mouth and do what I tell you, you'll become a winner." Of course, Steve had a lot to say to me, and we had a pretty good argument. But Steve learned.

In 1980 when Stone was a 25-game winner, he became a high-fastball pitcher. The hitters always were aware of his curve, so he was able to throw his fastball up high and right past them. Steve wasn't Goose Gossage, but his fastball was around 87 miles an hour, which was good enough, especially when the hitters were primarily worried about his curve. Steve was able to blow the ball right past good fastball hitters like Gorman Thomas and Cecil Cooper. Many would have you believe that a pitcher shouldn't throw a high fastball to Cooper or Thomas under any circumstances, but it can be a hell of a pitch.

I want my pitchers to call the game. It's the pitcher's game, and he is going to win or lose it. If a pitch doesn't work, the pitcher is the one who suffers the most. Let's go back to the example of the curveball pitcher whose curve isn't working. When I see that he doesn't have his curve, I tell him, not the catcher. The pitches he throws are his responsibility, and if the catcher keeps calling for the curve, the pitcher has to have sense enough to shake him off. Now, the pitcher may want to try and use his curve in a spot where it won't hurt him, in the hope of reestablishing the pitch. But he must know not to use the curve in a key part of the game. That isn't as easy as it sounds, because this pitcher has probably been getting out of jams for years thanks to his curve. Memories are a powerful thing, but common sense should prevail, and common sense should tell the pitcher to forget the curve for now.

Some pitchers do have complete faith in their catchers. Tippy Martinez will throw anything called by Rick Dempsey. The two played together with the Yankees and have known each other for

HEAD-HUNTING

I always spoke against beanballs. I didn't know for sure if some pitcher was throwing at hitters, but I always discouraged it. What good is hitting a batter and putting him on first base? The beanball is so dangerous. It has put people out of the game for life, deprived them of their livelihood.

I was beaned a number of times in the minors. The worst was when I was playing for New Orleans. I was wearing a batting helmet, but it didn't help, because I was hit under the left eye. The pitch crushed several bones. I remember that I had come up with the bases loaded. It was the first pitch to me, and it tailed right in. I tried to get out of the way, but the ball followed me. It was thrown by a sidearming right-hander who wanted to stay inside. It's a terribly helpless feeling: the more you lean back from the ball, the more it follows you. It's something you never forget. I don't believe it is right to endanger a man's life or his career by throwing at his head. It just isn't right.

But at the same time, a pitcher has to throw inside. Some hitters hang so close to home plate that it's impossible to pitch them on the outside corner. That's what they're looking for. To those guys a pitcher has to go for the inside corner. Carlton Fisk gets hit a number of times each season, because he stands right up on home plate and stays there as long as possible. His elbow is hanging over the plate, so if a fastball tails in, it could easily hit him. The pitcher has no intention of doing it. But pitchers are human. They can't stand sixty feet six inches away from the batter and throw every pitch exactly in the right spot. Sometimes the ball gets away from them. But I don't think there's any excuse for trying to hurt somebody with a pitch.

years. On the other hand, Jim Palmer will throw his own game. He'll shake off any catcher, because Jim knows exactly what he wants to do with each pitch and he isn't going to change his mind.

I like it when the pitcher moves the defense around. Jim Palmer did it, and it was always because he had something in mind. Jim might have gone into a game thinking he was going to pitch most hitters outside, so the defense would be set up to play the batters to the opposite field. But as the game went on, Jim might have switched to pitching inside. So he'd move the fielders to fit his revised pitching pattern. That's the sign of a thinking ballplayer.

We gave the Orioles the best information we had about where to pitch certain hitters and what their weaknesses were. Every pitcher was aware of this, and it was up to him to decide how he wanted to use this material. It's the pitcher's game. During his Cy Young Award year, Steve Stone didn't always pitch up high to the hitters who had trouble with high pitches. On some nights, Stone knew he wasn't throwing hard enough to go high in the strike zone. Pitchers have to be smart, because they're the ones in control.

The bullpen tends to take care of itself. As a manager, I went with the hot hand. Whoever was getting the job done for me in relief was the one I would use again and again, until he stopped getting out the hitters. Of course, you have to be careful not to overuse a pitcher. But a manager learns about his pitchers' arms. Tippy Martinez can throw a lot without it bothering him, so I used him often. That was not the case with some others. Tippy Martinez has the kind of arm that can bounce back day after day, and that's why he's making the good salary. Mike Flanagan could never go out and pitch in seventy or eighty games a year like Tippy. Neither could Scott McGregor. Physically, their arms couldn't stand the wear. When I used them in the bullpen during their rookie seasons, I made sure they had three days between appearances.

Sammy Stewart is another pitcher with a strong arm. He can pitch every other day or so and do the job. A big part of the Orioles' recent success was Sammy Stewart and his bionic arm. He can pitch in long relief and short relief, and he can start. He's there for whatever a manager needs. In my earlier years, the Orioles had Dick Hall and Moe Drabowsky, who could do the same thing.

WEAVER'S EIGHTH LAW

The best place for a rookie pitcher is long relief.

I believe young pitchers have to serve an apprenticeship, both for their own good and for the good of the team. The Orioles break in their rookie pitchers as long relievers. In 1975 Wayne Garland was 2–5. The next year he won twenty games. Dennis Martinez, Mike Flanagan, Scott McGregor, and about every other starting pitcher to come through our minor-league system began in long relief. If you have a good club, the prime objective is to win the pennant, and a manager doesn't experiment with kids. Not only is this first year a learning process for the pitcher, it's a learning process for the manager. The manager doesn't know what the pitcher can do in the majors. He has an idea and makes judgments about his talent, but a manager must see the pitcher in game conditions. When the manager puts a rookie pitcher into a game and the rookie comes through a few times, the manager begins evaluating. If Dennis Martinez has several good outings in long relief, then the manager must decide if the team would be better off with Martinez in the rotation, even if he has less experience than some other starter. It is a big responsibility and one of the toughest parts of managing.

A lot of people were surprised when I started Storm Davis in crucial games down the stretch in '82, including that last weekend series against the Brewers. But he'd shown me in his earlier work that he could do the job in relief, and I had enough faith in him to give him the start, and he came through with a clutch six-hitter.

If a rookie pitcher does very well in long relief and maybe in a few starts, at the end of the year the organization should clear a spot for him. That means you can trade one of your other starters. Over the years we were able to trade Mike Torrez, Rudy May, and Doyle Alexander because we had young pitchers to replace them. When Wayne Garland left us for free agency after winning twenty games in 1976, we weren't concerned because we thought Mike Flanagan could replace him. Flanagan had shown quite a bit as a rookie, even though he was 3–5 with a 4.13 ERA. Flanagan looked to me like he had the ability to be an effective major-league starter. Mike had a lot of trouble early in 1977. I stuck with him even though he began the year with a 2–8 record and many people were asking me how I could keep him in the rotation. I suffered with Mike, but he turned around and ended up that year 15–10, winning thirteen of his last fifteen decisions. Two years later he won twenty-three games and was voted the Cy Young Award. These are the moves a manager must make and stick with. The general manager can't make the decision, because the manager is closer to the situation.

I don't worry about having right-handers or left-handers in the bullpen. Why bring in a lefty to pitch to a left-handed hitter if that lefty pitcher can't do the job? Just because he's left-handed doesn't mean he automatically gets out left-handed hitters. It helps, but I stick with the hot hand, because usually he is getting out all the hitters—right-handers, left-handers, and switch-hitters. Put in the best guy you have to save the game. I see it as a day-to-day situation. The pitcher most likely to save the game for me that day is who I use. What he did last year or a month ago is beside the point. Often I'll start the year off with one pitcher as my main reliever and then switch to another. Recently, I alternated between Tippy Martinez and Tim Stoddard, depending upon who was throwing better. You have to be flexible in this area. Of course, if you have Goose Gossage in the bullpen, it's easy. But most teams don't have a guy who does the job year after year, like Gossage or Bruce Sutter.

The question of when to take out a pitcher is an interesting one. If the guy is getting hammered in the second inning and the game is getting out of hand, it's easy: the manager goes to the bullpen. But if the starter is struggling in the early innings while the score is still close, you've got to consider his history. Mike Cuellar often would get hit early in the game until he broke a sweat. Then he'd settle down and no one touched him. Knowing your players is the key.

There are no hard-and-fast rules for when to take out a pitcher late in the game, but there are a few pretty good clues:

HOW TO TELL IF A PITCHER IS LOSING HIS EDGE

1. **Pay attention to foul balls. When a pitcher gets in a good groove, the hitters will usually foul his deliveries straight back. There'll be plenty of foul tips. But if the hitters start making solid contact and belting the ball down the lines, watch out: they're catching up with the guy on the mound.**

2. **Watch the catcher.** Sometimes the catcher will give a knowing glance to the manager in the dugout, letting him know that the pitcher is not throwing as well as he has been.

3. **See if the pitcher continues to take the same amount of time between deliveries.** If he starts taking longer pauses as the game progresses, it's probably a sign that he's tired.

4. **Beware of leadoff walks.** If the pitcher has a three-run lead in the eighth inning and walks the first hitter on four straight pitches, it is probably an indication that he's tired. Every pitcher knows that this is the worst time to issue a walk. Therefore, he did it because of fatigue or a flaw in his motion.

5. **Watch the guys low in the order,** the hitters who usually hit the ball weakly or slap it to the opposite field. If they start pulling the ball, it's a sign of trouble.

6. **Watch where the pitches are going when they miss the strike zone.** If a sinkerball pitcher like Tommy John is wild high, odds are that he is not destined to spend a lot of time on the mound. But if he is wild low, there is probably little reason for concern.

7. **Watch the pitcher's delivery.** If it seems out of synch or if the pitcher appears to be falling down during his follow-through, there is probably something wrong. Jim Palmer has one of the most fluid motions the game has ever seen. If he should appear awkward, you know something is wrong.

I also use my statistics to decide on changing pitchers. Let's say it's a crucial part of the game, and Jim Palmer is pitching to Graig Nettles. Nettles is a .375 hitter against Palmer, but my stats show that he's only two for twenty-one against Tippy, so I'll bring in Martinez to face Nettles. The decision is made for you.

When I take a pitcher out, I'm concerned about the other team's possible pinch hitter. In the old days, a manager would not be wise to pull a lefty in order to bring in a right-handed relief pitcher against the Detroit Tigers, since the Tigers had Gates Brown sitting on the bench, just waiting for the chance to go up to the plate and win a game. A left-handed pinch hitter, Gates was one of the best ever in that role. So when you made a change, you had to be aware that Gates Brown was available. Would you rather have your left-handed starter pitch to the current hitter, and keep

Gates Brown on the bench, or should you take a chance and bring in a right-hander, and face Gates? I went to great lengths to keep Gates out of the game.

If you have some runs to play with, don't let the starter lose the game. Get him out before he has the chance to blow it. But if the score is 2–1 or 1–0, stick with your starter if he's throwing well. If the score is 4–1 in your favor and suddenly the starter has two men on and the winning run at the plate, you have to go to the bullpen. Even though the pitcher may not look as though he's out of gas, something must be going wrong. I've seen Dennis Martinez look awesome for six innings and then bang, bang, bang, they knock the heck out of him. He still looked strong. I'd check with the pitching coach and ask if Dennis was still throwing well. For five or six innings, Dennis would be eating up the hitters, but he would start throwing everything the same speed, and the hitters would adjust to him. A couple of hard-hit balls can tell you all you need to know about what a pitcher has left.

We keep track of how many times our pitchers warm up in the bullpen. You generally don't want them throwing for three straight days if you can help it, whether they get in the game or not. Some days a guy comes to the park and says he can't pitch in relief. Give him the night off, save his arm. Honesty between a relief pitcher and the manager is important. If a reliever feels too tired to pitch well, it doesn't do any good for him to take the mound. That's one way to lose a game. Tippy Martinez is good at this. He would come into the office after being in three straight games and maybe warming up the night before that and would say, "Earl, I just can't help you tonight," or "Earl, I can get you one batter and that's it." Communication means a lot.

When your pitching staff is beaten and your team gets into one of those ruts where you give up six or seven runs a game, the bullpen needs rest and you know it. The best way for that to happen is to get a complete game from the starting pitcher. But if the starters keep getting hit, you have to let a game go to something like 14–2. By that I mean a relief pitcher may have to stay out there and get pounded while the other pitchers rest. Or else you put in an outfielder like Larry Harlow or a catcher like Elrod Hendricks to pitch and finish up the game. I did that in Toronto in 1978, and some people acted as though it was the end of the world and I had somehow hurt the integrity of the game. Just about every team has done it since, and no one says anything. In a 162-game season, there are going to be those stretches. There's no way around it. It happened only once in fifteen years while I was with the Orioles. Don't misunderstand, before I brought in Harlow and Hendricks to pitch against Toronto, the Blue Jays had pounded seven of my pitchers for nineteen runs. They got only four off Harlow and Hendricks. When your pitching staff gives up nineteen runs, odds are it has ceased to be a ballgame. Some games just get out of hand, and then you have one of the most boring things in the world.

TEN PITCHERS ARE TOO MANY

I know a lot of teams carry ten pitchers on the roster, but I believe in going with eight or nine. I don't think a team needs any more, especially if the staff is relatively strong. With ten pitchers, one guy usually ends up rusting away. Rather than the tenth pitcher I'd rather have an extra player I could use to pinch-hit or maybe pinch-run. I believe that last regular player will help you win more games than a tenth pitcher. That extra player will be in the close games, while that extra pitcher will be on the mound in the blowouts.

If a team wants to get off to a fast start, they can go with three starting pitchers in April. That's all you need with an early-season schedule that features so many off days. But I was never really concerned about getting that fast start. I learned a long time ago that it's a long season, and I wanted everyone strong. Say I decided to start Palmer and Dennis Martinez in April. Then Scott McGregor and Mike Flanagan wouldn't be getting the work they needed to be prepared for the heavier schedule in late May and thereafter. Give all your players as many opportunities as possible early in the season, and they'll be ready to help you later when the real need is there.

One of my goals was to have the Orioles near the top of the league in fewest walks allowed. George Bamberger harped on it from the time he came to the park until the moment he left. I did the same thing. You keep talking about it because it's so important. The old baseball cliché that walks will kill you has a lot of truth to it.

Obviously, pitchers don't try to walk batters. Most of the time it's a matter of confidence. The pitcher needs confidence in his ability to get his stuff over the plate. Some pitchers get into the frame of mind in which they believe they must throw a perfect pitch. That isn't true. You can't just lob the ball down the middle, but you don't have to make a great pitch, or the perfect pitch, every time. The key to pitching is throwing the pitch the hitter isn't looking for. If you can do that, it doesn't have to be on the corners.

A successful pitcher must be able to get his breaking ball over the plate when the count is 2–1. The breaking ball or changeup thrown when a pitcher is behind in the count will often paralyze the hitter: it's the last thing he expects. Scott McGregor and Mike Flanagan have won a lot of games by throwing changeups with the count 2–0. Look, you tell your hitter to be ready for that inside fastball with a 2–0 count, to get the pitch he can really hit. It only makes sense to tell the pitcher not to throw it. But the pitcher must have a good breaking ball he can get over the plate. Furthermore, he must believe in his ability to control the pitch. Steve Stone reached the point where he could get his curve over any time, and he was striking out people on a high fastball when they were looking for a curve. And when they were sitting on the fastball, he fooled them with his curve. In a nutshell, that is the whole secret of pitching. It also is why the best hitters are successful only three of every ten at bats. The pitcher knows what he is going to throw, and the hitter doesn't.

Another thing that can help a pitcher is to cut down the time between pitches. A pitcher who takes an eternity between pitches on a cold day in April can really get to the defense. The players get stiff and their hands get cold and the defense suffers. Basically, a pitcher who works fast and gets the ball over the plate will stay in a good groove longer than a guy who walks all over the place and stares at the sky between pitches. The time for a pitcher to step off the mound and have a little talk with himself is when he gets wild or is getting hit. Then the pitcher should ask himself what he is doing wrong. His groove is gone, so taking that extra time won't hurt him.

There is an obvious time for a manager to go to the mound, and that is when the pitcher is getting hammered. Anyone knows that's when the manager has to go talk to the pitcher, to settle him down or take him out.

But there are other opportunities for someone to go to the mound and do some good. The manager and his pitching coach should know their pitchers and their motions inside and out. They should have a good idea exactly what each pitcher does when everything is going right and what bad habits he is prone to falling into. This comes from studying the pitchers so you can tell when they are overstriding or rushing their delivery. If you can pinpoint this problem soon enough and relay the information to the pitcher, who hopefully will make the proper adjustments, you can avoid a disaster.

When a manager or coach goes to the mound, nothing mysterious is taking place. Usually the manager will tell the pitcher if he saw something; maybe he's overstriding and that's why his pitches are high. Or the manager may want him to slow down a little, because he lost that good groove. So the manager tells him to relax, take his time. There also are occasions when the manager will ask the pitcher what he thinks is wrong and then discuss it with him. Of course, sometimes you just want to give the man in the pen a little more time to warm up before you bring him in.

Pitching is the most important, most delicate, and most challenging part of the game. You never have it all figured out. I remember a game when Aurelio Rodriguez was with the old Washington Senators and I had Mike Cuellar pitching. In the first inning Cuellar threw Rodriguez a fastball, and he homered. The next two times up, Cuellar got Rodriguez with screwballs. In the ninth inning Rodriguez batted again. Mike got two strikes on him and figured that Rodriguez would be looking for the screwball. Let's face it, the last thing a pitcher's going to do when he's ahead in the count like that is throw a fastball. So Mike crossed him up and threw a fastball. Rodriguez hit it over the center-field fence to beat us. Nothing in this game is a sure thing.

FIELDING

A Good Glove Is Worth
Its Weight in Gold

FIELDING is the most overlooked and maybe the least understood talent in baseball. Fans love to see diving stops and running catches, but the real key to fielding is anticipation and concentration. So many great running catches come when a fielder is making up for a bad jump on the ball. To me a great fielder is one who makes all the plays look simple.

Baltimore won a whopping total of thirty Gold Gloves in my fifteen years with the club. Of course, it helped to have such great players. Guys like Brooks Robinson, Mark Belanger, Bobby Grich, and Paul Blair were great fielders; in fact, it's hard to name players who ever played their positions any better. Their talent made them Gold Glove winners.

The Orioles were first or second in fielding percentage in thirteen of my fifteen seasons and were always known for executing fundamentals and not making costly errors. It helped to have the talent on the field. But our preparation made a big difference.

In their records the Orioles have a chart of every hitter's at bat against them since he came into the majors. If the player has been in the American League for a few years, you've got a pretty good line on him. That doesn't mean the hitter will always hit the ball where you position the fielders, but you have enough information to get your defense in the right spots. With a record of every at bat against Baltimore, you can look back and see trends. Some guys always hit a low fastball up the middle and always pull a changeup. So common sense tells you to have your fielders shade up the middle if the pitcher is using his fastball or play the hitter to pull if the pitcher is going to his changeup.

A good pitching chart will also tell you the count of the pitch that was hit, what kind of pitch was hit, and where the pitch was hit. After a number of years a manager knows where a guy should hit the ball. That's information for your pitchers and fielders. If a player such as Gorman Thomas has hit only two balls to right field in six years, you have to give him the right-field line.

I never worried about where batters hit the ball against other teams, only where they hit it against the Orioles. To break it down even further, we'd track where each ball went against each pitcher, because players might hit the ball in one place against Jim Palmer and in the opposite place against Scott McGregor.

All infielders need the same basic skills: good hands, good eye-hand coordination, agility, and quickness of feet and hands. Each position has its own special demands, but dependable hands and quick feet are needed at all spots. Infielders need the ability to move left and right—that's where they get their range. They have to be able to move in swiftly to handle a slow hit ball. A good infielder always charges in to take away a hit off a slow roller.

But it's more than physical attributes. It takes knowledge of the game. The infielders should know when the opposition might bunt and be looking for a steal with someone like Rickey Henderson on first base. An infielder must keep things straight. He has to remember what base to cover in a particular bunt situation, where to go if the runner is stealing or if the ball is hit to the outfield. Of course, a player receives plenty of help and instruction from the manager, and each manager has his own method of handling each game situation. But the point I want to make is that the infielder must *know* where he is to go on every single play, and he has to know it without even thinking about it. If one guy forgets to cover a base or blows an assignment, it can cost a team the ball game. These mistakes are made at all levels, even in the World Series. A

ORIOLES GOLD GLOVE WINNERS UNDER WEAVER

1970	Brooks Robinson	3b		1975	Mark Belanger	ss
	Dave Johnson	2b			Bobby Grich	2b
	Paul Blair	of			Paul Blair	of
1971	Brooks Robinson	3b			Brooks Robinson	3b
	Mark Belanger	ss				
	Dave Johnson	2b		1976	Mark Belanger	ss
	Paul Blair	of			Bobby Grich	2b
					Jim Palmer	p
1972	Brooks Robinson	3b				
	Paul Blair	of		1977	Mark Belanger	ss
1973	Brooks Robinson	3b			Jim Palmer	p
	Mark Belanger	ss				
	Bobby Grich	2b		1978	Mark Belanger	ss
	Paul Blair	of			Jim Palmer	p
1974	Brooks Robinson	3b				
	Mark Belanger	ss		1979	Jim Palmer	p
	Bobby Grich	2b				
	Paul Blair	of		1982	Eddie Murray	1b

lapse of concentration can be more costly than letting a ground ball go through your legs.

Every infielder needs to be able to move laterally. By that I mean breaking to the left or right. It requires peripheral vision, and the more an infielder can see out of the corners of his eyes, the wider his field of vision and the better he's able to keep track of everything on the diamond. In order to move laterally a player must have his weight distributed evenly on the balls of his feet. He should not be leaning forward or back but have his weight divided equally on each foot as the ball is released by the pitcher.

An infielder must make his first move to his right or left, not forward or backward. A ball hit directly at a player will be within reach no matter where he goes with his first step. His primary concern is reaching the ball hit six feet to his right or left. As the pitch heads toward the plate, the infielder can see if it'll be inside or outside. A good infielder will watch the pitcher release the ball and then concentrate on the hitter, seeing where the hitter wants to hit the pitch. Is the hitter trying to pull it or slap it to the opposite field? Suppose there is a right-handed hitter at the plate and the pitch is outside. Everyone should be leaning left, since he's likely to hit the ball to right field. If the pitch is inside, the infielders should lean to their right, since he's likely to pull it.

If everyone's doing their job in the infield, they all should be leaning in the same direction when the ball goes past the hitter. That's something to watch for during games, to see if the defense is thinking together. It won't necessarily be the right way—a hitter might surprise you by pulling an outside pitch—but everyone should be going the same way.

WEAVER'S NINTH LAW

The key step for an infielder is the first one—to the left or right, but *before* the ball is hit.

Say Gorman Thomas is the hitter. If the pitch is inside, the third baseman should be taking a step toward the bag, the short-stop a step toward the left-field line, the second baseman a step to his right, and the first baseman a step toward the second baseman. The infield is playing smart and in sync. Now, Thomas may go inside-out with that inside pitch and hit it to the opposite field, fooling everyone. But that doesn't mean the defense was out of position; it's just one of those things that happens. This skill of taking the first step in the right direction is something that can be learned at any level of baseball. It is a good way of increasing a player's range, because he's already going in the right direction in most instances when the ball is hit. Experience is important here, because the infielders need not only to see the pitch but also to be able to judge where it's going to cross the plate.

The infielders should know what pitch is being thrown because they can see the catcher's signals. If Jim Palmer is pitching and Rick Dempsey calls for a curveball to Thomas on the outside cor- ner, then the infielders should be leaning to their left. That first step always should be lateral, not forward or back. You want to make sure you get the ball on the best possible hop. The further away from the last hop you catch the ball, the better. If every ball were caught belt-high after it bounced, there never would be an error. The short hops, where you catch the ball a fraction of a second after it hits the ground, are the toughest plays. Try to get the ball on the highest possible hop.

Avoid short hops whenever possible. Now, if a player with speed, like Rickey Henderson or Tim Raines, hits a high hopper, the fielder has to get to it as soon as possible, and that may mean catching it on a short hop. The speedsters get down the line extremely quickly, and an infielder has no time to waste. Most errors are made when there is a high hopper and the infielder has to charge in and tries to take it on the short hop.

It sounds very basic, but the only way to learn how to handle balls on the best possible hop is to have someone hit you grounder after grounder, or field as many balls as possible during batting practice. It comes down to hard work and practice. As you get experienced, you can look at a ball and see how the hops will be. Usually you can tell if the ball will stay low and skid on you or if it will bounce high. In spring training Brooks Robinson and Mark Belanger would take a hundred ground balls a day. When they first broke in, they took even more. I've heard of some players who handled a thousand grounders a day. There are no short cuts to becoming a good fielder. When I was growing up, I would take as many ground balls as anyone would hit me. Usually I wore out the guy hitting me the grounders. A lot of big leaguers did the same thing when they were young.

What follows is a look at the special demands of each position.

First Base

Until a runner reaches first, the first baseman is just another infielder; his main concern is to be ready for a ground ball. The moment the ball is hit anywhere but to him, he's got to move quickly to the base and straddle the bag, once again with his weight evenly distributed. If the throw is to his left, he touches the bag with his right foot while stretching out toward the throw with his left foot. If the throw is to the right, his left foot hits the bag and the stretch is done with his right foot. If the throw is right at him, he can keep either foot on the bag.

One of the toughest plays for a first baseman is the high throw that's heading behind him, going into the runner. For this throw the first baseman moves *behind* the bag into foul territory. His first job is to catch the ball. Once that's accomplished, then he should touch the back corner of the base, the one on the foul line, with whatever foot is most comfortable. When a first baseman goes across the base for the high throw, it will slow the runner up because he'll naturally want to avoid a collision, particularly when you consider the size of most first basemen.

When a runner is on first, the first baseman should stand with his feet comfortably apart, his weight balanced, one foot up against the base, and the other foot in fair territory, on a line with the pitcher. When the pitcher throws to first, the first baseman should step back to straddle the base, a foot on each side of the bag. When the throw comes, he can catch it and put the tag right down on the runner. A lot of first basemen just keep the one foot on the bag, catch the throw, and try to slap back with the tag. The umpire rarely calls the runner out on this type of tag. But when the first baseman is straddling the bag, he catches the ball in perfect position to make the tag. The runner slides into the tag, and the umpire is far more likely to call him out. By straddling the bag and having the ball right over the base, there is no way the runner can avoid the tag.

It doesn't make any difference if the first baseman is a right-hander or a left-hander. Boog Powell was an excellent fielder, and he was right-handed. Eddie Murray, also a right-hander, is a superb fielder. Jim Spencer was a fine first baseman, and he was left-handed. A lefty has one advantage: when a ground ball is hit to him, he doesn't have to turn to throw to second base. On that play the right-hander has to pivot around to make the throw. A left-hander can make the play a little faster because he catches the ball and comes up throwing.

But all in all which arm a player throws with has nothing to do with his defensive skills at first. A player will be as good as he wants to, if he's willing to put in the work and practice, practice, practice. I believe Eddie Murray has become the best fielding first baseman in the majors. He covers more ground than anyone else at the position, his lateral movement is amazing, and he keeps his weight balanced and on the balls of his feet as the pitcher winds up. His footwork is superb, so you never see him tying himself up in knots while trying to stretch for a throw.

Eddie's also great at charging in and fielding bunts, another very demanding play. With a runner on first and the hitter in an obvious sacrifice situation, the first baseman's chief concern is to hold the runner close. He can't be charging in for the bunt until the ball is delivered to home plate. You don't want that runner getting a big lead because then he can steal second or at least get such a huge jump that it's almost impossible to force him at second, even on a poor bunt. My teams used a set of signs for these spots. For example, the first baseman may take off his glove for a moment. That could mean that the pitcher should make exactly two pickoff throws to first, but that after the two throws, the first baseman is charging in for the bunt. Another sign might tell the pitcher to forget the pickoff, because the first baseman is charging on the play. Each team and manager have their own set of signs for the various options. All of them are designed to keep that runner close to the bag.

With runners on first and second in a bunt situation, the first baseman doesn't really have to hold the runner on, since the runner at first has nowhere to go. The first baseman can play in front of the runner and can start creeping in as the pitcher starts his motion to the plate. In this situation the first baseman's primary duty is to try and catch the ball and throw it to third to force the runner from second.

There's one thing about the bunt: the defensive team can't stop an excellent sacrifice bunt. If the ball is bunted slowly down one of the foul lines, it's virtually impossible to throw out the lead runner. Then, the defense should be content to get the runner at first. Make sure to get at least one out rather than gambling and not retiring anyone.

Second Base and Shortstop

The second baseman and the shortstop have a lot in common. They've got a lot of ground to cover, so their primary concern is being able to move laterally to keep ground balls from getting past them. They also need to learn to play the ball on the correct hop and to make a good, strong, accurate throw to first.

But the main function of the second baseman and shortstop is turning the double play. There's an old saying that a double play is the pitcher's best friend. Well, it's that and much more. It's the defensive team's best weapon. Nothing cuts the heart out of a rally faster than a double play. When I had Mark Belanger at short teaming first with Dave Johnson, then with Bobby Grich, and later with Rich Dauer, they seldom failed to execute a double play. And they were quick enough to turn some ground balls into two outs where others would have been lucky to get even a force play. A good team must have a reliable double-play combination. If the double plays aren't made, it puts too much extra pressure on the pitching staff.

Any time there's a runner at first and less than two outs, you look for the double play. The shortstop and second baseman should leave their normal positions and move toward second by a few steps. They want to make sure they can cover the base and start the double play. That may give the hitter a little larger hole in the infield through which he can hit the ball, but the risk is worth taking. The middle infielder must be able to get to second in plenty of time, because he might get a bad throw and he'll need his balance to catch it. Also, the man pivoting at second on the double play must have his body under control so he can catch the ball, make the throw to first, and get out of the way of the sliding runner. I always stressed to my players that their first job was to get at least one out. If the throw to second is a poor one, forget about turning the double play. If necessary, go off the bag to catch the throw and then come back to the base and get the force out. Believe me, one out is better than none. A double play will kill a rally, but a botched double play, where everyone is safe, is like pouring the proverbial gasoline on a fire. Not only does the team in the field fail to get the one out, but it also feels disappointed about it, and the team at bat feels as though it's been given an extra out. You always have to get one out.

There are many ways to turn the double play, and many players develop their own style. Manny Trillo has a half-dozen pivots and always throws sidearm. Willie Randolph also has a number of pivots, but his throws are mostly overhand. The basics are the ability to catch the ball, touch the base, get out of the way of the runner, and make a strong, sure throw to first base. If you fail to touch the base, don't stop and step back; rather, continue a fluid motion and throw to first. The umpire may not have noticed that the bag wasn't touched. If the infielder stops and steps back, it becomes clear, and he might not get anyone out. But I do *not* believe in teaching infielders to cheat by making the phantom tag at second. Some managers tell infielders to take their feet off the base as they catch the ball to save them an extra second on the pivot and the throw to first. I am *totally* against this. You leave yourself wide open to be hurt by an umpire's call, and I hate to be in that precarious situation. I want the umps to call the game as clean and as strict as they can; that's what I keep reminding them from the dugout. I don't want any team to get away with that phantom tag against me, so I make sure my fielders don't use it. That's a part of fundamentals, too.

There are some cases where the middle infielder can't play too close to second. For example, the second baseman must play over toward first if there is a left-handed pull hitter like Jason Thompson at bat. He must guard that hole between first and second. The same is true for the shortstop if there's a right-handed pull hitter like Andre Thornton at the plate. Thornton will hit a lot of balls in the hole between second and third. The shortstop has to be in position to cover the area. Once again, this requires good preparation on the part of the team. The manager and the coaching staff have to keep the infielders informed of where certain batters are likely to hit the ball. The Orioles always kept track of this information. We had a card on every hitter that told us how he should be pitched and where he was likely to hit the ball.

When I managed the Orioles, I had three excellent second basemen in Johnson, Grich, and Dauer. Each had a very strong arm for a second baseman, and that was a big plus on the double play. When they took the throw from the shortstop or third baseman, they could really get something on the throw to first. Having a good arm isn't necessary to play second, but it sure helps. A second baseman can get by with a weaker arm than a third baseman or shortstop, but a good arm is still a plus at the position. Of course, if I had a second baseman who could hit .290 with 20 homers, I wouldn't worry much about his arm. He wouldn't turn as many double plays, but his bat would make up for it.

I love to watch Rich Dauer play second. Here's a guy who

went through half the 1978 season—86 straight games—without making an error. It's a tremendous achievement. The key is great concentration. Rich knows how to play the ball correctly. He gets it on the proper hop and always seems to know how he will catch it. He makes his mind up quickly and is kind of a throwback in that he's more than willing to knock down a ground ball with his body. He'll go down on one knee to make sure his body is in front of the ball and that the grounder doesn't get away from him. You can't do this on a double play, but with no one on base there is nothing wrong with a second baseman taking a ground ball on one knee. At second base, you have time to go down on one knee because of the shorter throw. A third baseman and shortstop don't have that luxury. Granted, a lot of guys don't go down on one knee any more, but then a lot of guys make errors at second, and many of them come from carelessness. Now, if Rickey Henderson or Omar Moreno hits a grounder to second, their quickness probably means that the second baseman won't have time to go down on one knee, make the play, get up, and then throw to first base. The one-knee maneuver is a good one, but the speed of the runner must always be considered.

A shortstop needs the same basic ingredients as a second base-man: good range, dependable hands, and a knowledge of how to play the grounders on the proper hop. But he needs a much better arm, because his throw to first base is longer. Also, he doesn't have time to go down on one knee to catch a grounder. The short-stop has to charge more balls than the second baseman does. He can't afford to wait for the ball to reach him and still expect to throw out the runner at first base. If a shortstop backs up on a ground ball, he gives the runner an extra three steps going to first. A shortstop can do that on some slow runners, but not usually.

When a shortstop is charging a slow roller, I want him to catch the ball with the glove and then throw to first. A lot of players try to go after the ball with their bare hand so they can make a quicker throw. But this do-or-die play leads to many mistakes. Trying to run in and catch the ball with the bare hand and make a throw to first is very demanding, and I think it's too risky. I like the short-stop to come in, get the glove in front of him, catch the ball, and then make a strong and true throw to first. If the throw is a little late, that's the way it goes; at least he gave it a good shot. But if he runs in, tries to pick up the ball with his bare hand, and drops it, he never had a chance.

Like a second baseman, a shortstop should have several different double-play pivots. These are things that come through practice. Players have to find pivots that are comfortable for them, pivots that enable them to get out of the way of the runner and still make a decent throw to first base.

Mark Belanger always made far fewer errors than the average shortstop. Like Dauer, Belanger had great concentration and knew how to play the hops. And as with Dauer, that came from a lot of time on the practice field and a willingness not to take any play for granted. These guys never assumed they would make the play. They didn't take their eyes off the ball or go to make a throw before the ball was securely in their gloves. They made sure every little thing was done right.

Belanger also spent plenty of time getting his legs loose so he could bend way down and keep his glove on the ground. Mark always kept the glove at ground level. It's much easier to lift up the glove to catch a high bouncer than it is to bring the glove down to handle that ground-skimmer. You often see balls go right through an infielder's legs, and it happens everywhere from Little League to the majors. The reason is that the infielder doesn't have his glove at ground level: he's holding it high, and the ball scoots right under. Mark's first rule was to keep the glove as low as possible.

Mark was always very cool in the field. Some ground balls take one big hop, and shortstops charge them and try to make the grab just as soon as they start their second hop. That's a risky play. Mark had the marvelous ability to let the ball take the first hop and then charge in and catch it in the middle of the second hop and throw to first all in one motion. This enabled him to play that second big hop rather than try to take the ball on the short hop. It's a little thing, but it often is the difference between making the play and making an error.

I believe every infielder must go after every ground ball with the thought that it's going to take a bad hop. Then, if the ball does take an unexpected bounce, the infielder is ready to make the adjustment quickly. But if he goes after the ball figuring it'll be a routine play, his mind and body won't be able to adapt if that ground ball suddenly flattens out and hugs the grass or if it takes a high hop. If he keeps his body flexible and loose and if his hands are down low below the ball, he'll make the play. In other words, expect the bad hop and be ready for the worst. When it happens, you can adjust. If the ball takes its normal hop, you'll make the play with no sweat. Once again, it's all concentration.

Mark Belanger used a very small glove, but I don't think this is necessary. The selection of the glove is up to the individual. The key is comfort. Mark liked a small glove, but generally I believe that the bigger the glove the better. The small glove helped Mark get the ball out and on its way to first very fast on a double play. The ball never got stuck in the webbing, and it worked great for him. But a larger glove will give you a larger area in which to catch the ball. It should enable you to catch more ground balls. The larger glove may make it a little more difficult to get rid of the ball on the double play, but it shouldn't be much trouble once you get used to it.

Third Base

A third baseman doesn't have to be fast like a sprinter, but he needs to be quick and have good reactions. Lateral movement is so important. Brooks Robinson was the best I've ever seen at having his weight balanced and at knowing which way to lean as the pitch approached the hitter. If there was a right-handed batter up and the pitch was inside, Brooks would be leaning toward the third-base line. Leaning in the proper direction really helped him get the fast first step that led to his making those amazing plays to his left and right. Brooks also had a very accurate arm.

Aurelio Rodriguez had one of the strongest arms around, and this enabled him to play deeper at third than some others. He could get the ball over to first so quickly that he could sometimes wait for an extra hop. That's as much an advantage at third as at anywhere else in avoiding tough hops. Most players don't have a Rodriguez arm. But a third baseman with a great arm has a big advantage.

What made Brooks Robinson so outstanding was that he got to the ball fast, had wonderful hands, and made his throws to first extremely quickly. In other words, he did not hang on to the ball for very long. Another aspect of Brooks's greatness was that he played the bunt better than anyone I have ever seen and probably better than anyone who has ever or will ever play the game. Brooks could charge at the batter at full speed and never have to slow down to make the play. When most third basemen charge in and field a bunt, they field it with their weight on their left foot. This way, they have their balance. It's the standard method, but it also means taking one more step to throw the ball to first base, since a right-hander can't make a throw with his weight on his left foot. Just try it sometime.

But Brooks somehow taught himself to come roaring in for the bunt and field it on his *right* foot and throw to first all in one motion. I've never seen anything like it. Brooks actually fielded the bunt with his bare hand about a step *behind* the ball. That is, he ran up next to the ball, reached back, grabbed it, and threw while standing on one foot. How can you teach that? Every other player needs that one last step for the throw. Everyone but Brooks. Others have tried to copy Brooks, but it's never worked. It's simply great instincts and great ability, and it's part of what made Brooks Robinson unique.

Like all infielders, the third baseman must be able to handle pop-ups. The first thing to remember is to have sunglasses if you're playing a day game. A pop-up coming out of the sun is a wicked play. If you can't see the ball, how can you catch it? When a pop-up is hit behind you, move quickly back and get positioned under the ball so that you have time to plant your feet and keep your balance. Of course, you can't do this every time, but it's something to shoot for. One tough play for the third baseman and for the first baseman is the pop-up hit in foul territory near the stands. On this play the infielder should get to the stands as fast as possible, then come back toward the playing field if he overran the ball. This way he knows where the stands are and how far he can go. Sometimes an infielder can't help but crash into the stands. But that's a dangerous play and a good way to get hurt.

The Outfield

Defensively the key here is speed. An outfielder has so much territory to cover that the faster he is, the easier it will be for him to reach balls hit down the lines and in the alleys. But you also want your outfielders to be able to hit, so you're much more willing to accept a bad fielder in the outfield than in the infield. That's why you see some slower players in the outfield. They make up for that lack of speed with home runs and RBIs or a high batting average. Naturally every manager is looking for another Frank Robinson or Willie Mays, guys who can do it all.

An outfielder also needs a strong arm, because his throw to the infield is a long one. A good arm will stop runners from taking an extra base, and maybe from scoring from third on a short fly ball.

It begins to sound like a broken record, but the only way to improve is to practice. An outfielder can refine his skills every day during batting practice. He can take his position and catch all the balls hit in his direction. The balls hit in batting practice are the same type that will come his way during the game, and the only way to learn how to judge fly balls and line drives is to catch thousands of them. Having a coach hit you fly balls off a fungo bat is also good practice.

Instinct and natural talent mean quite a bit. Paul Blair could stand in center field and know when a ball was hit over his head. He would turn around and run, never looking back at the ball, get to a spot, and then look up—and there would be the ball. He'd grab it easily. No one can explain what Paul Blair had that gave him the ability to run and run and then know exactly where the ball was coming down. That's something that can't be learned. Such players know where the ball is going long before it gets there. Watching them, it seems they know as soon as the ball leaves the bat. It can't be explained or taught.

But some things can be learned. The outfielder's first responsibility is to get to the ball. Don't take it easy and then try to reach back and make a catch over your shoulder. It may look nice, but it's too risky. If your judgment is slightly off, the ball is over your head. The good outfielder runs hard until he's under the ball, plants his feet, and makes the safe catch. Catching the ball at the last second also leaves you vulnerable if the wind should suddenly kick up. That can be enough to push the ball out of your reach.

An outfielder, like an infielder, should have his weight balanced. He also should be leaning on the pitch if he can see that it's going to be inside or outside. Most players, even from the outfield, can see the ball going over the plate and so are able to lean in the proper direction.

It's great to have a center fielder like Paul Blair because he can cover so much ground. But that doesn't give the manager a green light to play extremely poor fielders in left and right. Those guys still have to handle balls hit at them and near the lines.

Some outfielders like to play shallow. They believe they can cut down on singles by catching the balls hit just over the infield. But this leaves them open to being beaten on the deep fly ball to the fence. I don't like outfielders to play shallow. For the most part, it's asking for trouble. If there's a runner on first and the outfield is playing deep, the odds are against the runner scoring unless the hitter really belts it. That deep outfield might give up a single in front of them, allowing the runner to go to second, but it won't allow the double that scores a run. A shallow outfield, on the other hand, might allow that runner to score from first on a deep fly ball, because they probably won't reach it and it'll go for extra bases. Also, a shallow outfield is more vulnerable to having line drives hit between them and rolling to the fence. A right fielder and a center fielder playing at normal depth will get to a liner hit between them on one or two bounces and will hold the hitter to a single, but that same line drive reaches the fence against a shallow outfield. The shallow outfield gives up a double or a triple in the hope of cutting off a bloop single. To me this doesn't make much sense. Also, an outfielder playing at normal depth will have time to get back to the fence and maybe make a leaping catch of a fly ball that might otherwise go out of the park for a homer. An out-fielder playing shallow never even reaches the fence and has no chance to take away the homer.

When setting up the outfield, it helps to have a guy with speed and great natural ability in center field. Some people want a differ-ent type of player in right field than in left. To me it doesn't matter. Sure, it's nice to have a guy with a strong arm in right so he can throw out that runner who's going from first to third on a base hit to right. But if the guys in right and left are hitting for you and not killing you on defense, you can run the risk of allowing the runner to take that extra base. It's not an ideal situation, but a manager is always weighing a player's defense against his offense to determine if he should be in the lineup. I don't think that the occasional extra

base is worth sacrificing much offense for, except in the late innings when I'm protecting a lead.

Catcher

A catcher needs the agility to be able to shift his weight quickly
right or left to catch pitches. He also needs courage. More than
any other player, he cannot be afraid to put his body in front of the
ball to block it. Stopping a 90-mile-an-hour fastball in the dirt takes
some guts. And the catcher must get his body in front of it—
sticking out his glove isn't enough. Also, the catcher must be willing to hold his ground when a throw is coming from the outfield
and a runner is trying to score. That runner is coming full speed,
but the catcher can't give ground when making the tag. He has to
be fearless. He has to be willing to let the ball hit him in the shin
guards, the chest protector, or just about anywhere on his body.

The better the arm, the more likely it is that a catcher will be
able to throw out base runners trying to steal. But a catcher
doesn't need a great arm; he needs a pitcher who will watch the
runner on base and keep the runner near the bag by throwing over
there. Thurman Munson never had a great arm, but he had an
accurate arm, he could get rid of the ball quickly, and he played
for a team loaded with left-handed pitchers who kept the runners
close. Rick Dempsey and Jim Sundberg have terrific arms. But the
greatest arm in the world won't help a catcher when the runner is
halfway to second base before the ball gets to home plate.

A catcher can't really improve the strength of his arm much.
For the most part, either you have a strong arm or you don't. But
a catcher can practice catching the ball, getting it out of his glove,
and throwing it *fast*. A big, slow arm motion on the throw will
negate a strong arm. Every team works on having its catchers
improve their defense, and much progress can be made. When he
came to the Orioles, Elrod Hendricks was not a good defensive
catcher. But he became one by working with the coaches, working
on his own, and basically working whenever he got the chance. He
practiced and practiced his throwing, experimenting to find the
quickest release that still permitted him to have a strong, accurate
throw. He had coaches throw one-bouncers in front of him so he
could practice blocking balls in the dirt.

As I said before, it helps if the pitcher and catcher are of the same mind and can work together when calling a game. It's a great situation when the pitcher is thinking that he wants to throw a curve and the catcher puts down two fingers. But it's up to the pitcher to call his own game. When a catcher calls for a pitch, it's just a suggestion. The pitcher makes the final decision, since he's the one who is throwing the ball and it's his game. I don't believe a catcher must be able to "call a good game." It is a plus but not a necessity.

Blocking the plate is another part of the catcher's job. It takes plenty of courage. The catcher should position himself toward the third-base corner of the plate. He must remember that his main job is to catch the ball first and then make the tag. You see a lot of catchers going for the tag before they have possession of the ball. If the catcher has to move from the corner of the plate to get the throw, then he should move: blocking the plate is worthless without the ball.

Once he has the ball, the catcher should hold it in his bare hand, and that hand should be tucked inside his glove. That way, the ball will be protected when he goes to make the tag, and there will be less of a chance of it coming loose when the runner slides into him. The catcher has every right to block the plate if he has the ball. You can teach the technique, but you can't teach the guts it takes to stand there while a runner comes charging at you.

PLAYERS

Never Promise a Rose Garden
Or a Starting Job

A MANAGER should stay as far away as possible from his players: no personal contact with the players in the clubhouse or off the field. I don't know if I said ten words to Frank Robinson while he played for me. I didn't have to. We were friendly—always said hello and so on. But I'm talking about lengthy conversations. We didn't have any. I don't think Frank expected it. All I could hope for was that Frank would go out and do his job the way he was supposed to. And each day he did just that. The same holds true for Brooks Robinson, Boog Powell, and Lee May. With these guys I might have shared a joke or two in an airplane, but in the clubhouse there were no words, no private conferences, nothing. I wrote their names in the lineup, and they played to the best of their ability.

When a manager can walk through the clubhouse and enter his office and then sit there by himself, he knows he has a pretty good ballclub. When there is no one knocking at the door and he doesn't have to tell a coach to send so-and-so into the office after he arrives, then he has a happy team.

We traded for Ken Singleton before the 1975 season. That first spring I didn't even know Kenny was around, because he went everywhere he was told to. He knew how to follow directions and was dedicated to getting his work in.

Earl Williams was a different story. When Baltimore picked him up from Atlanta in 1973, we had our hands full. That first spring we were always chasing him around the field. It was, "Earl, you're supposed to be catching," or "Earl, it's your turn to hit," or "Earl, you're supposed to be blocking balls in the dirt." It never ended.

That is why the less you talk to a player, the better off everyone will be. Of course, these are my personal beliefs, and other managers have been successful being close to their players. I'd say that I might even be by myself in some of my feelings about the separation between a manager and his players, but I know it worked for me.

To my mind the situation is this: if you do a lot of joking with the players in hotel lobbies or on airplanes, then they are liable to start thinking you're joking around at the park, and things can get out of control. The players wonder how you can be such a nice guy away from the park and such a jerk in the dugout when you have to give them an order. That's the last thing I wanted the players to say.

Frank Robinson and Brooks Robinson were a dream to manage. Frank always was where he should be. Brooks would be one of the last guys to arrive at the park, but the minute he pulled on that uniform, you could see he was going to have a good time that night. He'd be on the field exactly on time for infield practice. Lee May was the same way, and so is Eddie Murray, and this business-like attitude carries through the team. These guys lead by example.

Eddie Murray is much more than a great player. He is very professional in his approach to the game. He doesn't like to talk to the manager very much, and he never gives a manager problems. The less Eddie talks, the better off he is. He likes to joke around with the people around his locker, but he doesn't seem comfortable joking with the manager. It's a different relationship between a player and a player than between a player and the manager. Sooner or later, there comes a time when the manager has to correct a player. You don't want the player to say, "How can this guy look me in the eye one day and be so nice and then the next day do something like this to me?"

This sort of employee-employer relationship is something I've known all my life. It didn't come from anyone I played under; to me it just seems like the proper way to do things. You know the old saying, familiarity breeds contempt. There's some truth to it in this context.

That might not hold true for someone with a different personality. Some managers have done well being buddy-buddy with their players. But I do know this: if you haven't slapped a guy on the back and told him what a great person and player he is, then it's much easier when the day comes and you have to call him into the office and tell him he screwed up.

I'm not going to make any promises. That was one of my methods of dealing with players. No promises. None. If you don't make any promises, then you won't break any. Don't back yourself into a corner.

I've met people from all walks of life, going back to my days in the minors when I carried the hod, sold used cars, and worked for Liberty Loan. Meeting people from every segment of society means a lot, because ballplayers are such a diverse group. You run into all sorts of people playing ball, the kid from Alabama who dropped out of the sixth grade and the pitcher from Harvard. Ballplayers come from all fifty states, from families with millions and from families on welfare and from everywhere in between. You run into people like Mike Epstein, who wanted to convince you that he knew something about Socrates. You run into guys who just want to go out and get into fights. You can't put people into categories. No matter what they're like, my job is to get the most out of them as players.

Take Boog Powell. The only thing I ever told Boog to do was to drop some weight, and the only reason I brought it up was that my general manager had suggested it. I mentioned the weight to Boog, but I knew he was happiest at a high weight. He was one crabby man when he couldn't eat. A lot of big people get very unhappy when they can't eat what they like. When Boog was eating all he wanted, he was much happier and generally played better. I believe he was a fine player no matter what he weighed.

He was the Most Valuable Player in the American League in 1970 at 270 pounds. Some people wanted him to get down to 240, but he felt that made him weak. Boog might have been right. A big guy like Tim Stoddard or Boog can drop five to ten pounds without it hurting, but when these fellows lose thirty pounds, it makes a big difference.

Jim Palmer and I had a relationship based on mutual respect. That doesn't mean we always agreed. Nor does it mean that we were never angry with each other. Jim and I were very honest with each other. We said what was on our minds, and sometimes the words stung.

Often our disagreements centered on how much Jim should pitch. There were times that Jim wanted to come out of a game and I wanted him to stay on the mound. But these were sincere differences of opinion about what was best for the Orioles—Jim felt a reliever would be more likely to get out of the jam. Obviously, Jim knew his own body better than anyone else, so you had to respect his opinion.

Jim is a perfectionist. He wants every pitch to be in the exact spot he's selected. He wants to feel 100 percent healthy before he takes the mound. In other words, he wants to feel his best so he can give his best. Sometimes, I suggested that he pitch even though he wasn't 100 percent, as long as he wouldn't further injure himself.

OK, there were times when we were upset with each other, but we never held grudges. What's more, Jim pitched like a Hall of Famer for me. He kept himself in tremendous shape and was a great example for young pitchers. When they saw Jim Palmer doing his running and exercises, they knew that you can't take anything for granted in this game.

Good players are never complacent. They strive to improve. And they do. Look at what Steve Stone did after he joined the Orioles. You *can* teach an old dog some new tricks.

A veteran pitcher can learn a new wrinkle. He wants to win, so he will learn. George Bamberger was very good at helping veteran pitchers add another pitch. You ought to be able to teach someone who has matured faster than someone who has not. You'll find that a lot of guys who know it all after their second or third year in the big leagues discover they don't know so much after seven years.

Players have to learn how to adjust in order to stay in the majors. Take Dan Graham. He came to Baltimore in 1980 and had a super season: in 266 at bats he had 15 homers and batted .278. He was a left-handed-hitting catcher with power, and there aren't too many of them around. But the next year the pitchers started eating him up. They got the book on him. They learned what they could do to him, and he couldn't stop it. They threw off-speed pitches on the outside part of the plate, and he was lost. For half of 1981 he kept saying, "I took care of it last year, I'll be all right." But in 1980 they hadn't given him those off-speed pitches outside. Now he was getting a steady diet of them. When he finally agreed to make some changes, he still had problems. By the end of the season, he had hit only .176 with just two homers, and he was out of the majors.

Every player goes through a period of adjustment, but some players don't have any big weaknesses. Al Kaline came out of high school and didn't quit playing for the Tigers until he had 3,000 hits. I'm sure Kaline went through some slumps, but you know he had a lot fewer weaknesses than Dan Graham. You also know that a guy like Al Kaline was intelligent enough to be very aware of how the pitchers were working him and to make the necessary adjustments to deal with those changes.

A guy who learned how to survive and who made a good career for himself was Al Bumbry. First, Al started his career late because he was a platoon leader in Vietnam after graduating from Virginia State. His minor-league career really didn't start until he was twenty-four, so he had to make it fast, and he paid the price through hard work and sweat.

Bumbry came up to Baltimore in 1973 as a twenty-six-year-old rookie, and he hit .337 with a league-leading 11 triples. I platooned him to a certain extent that first season, keeping him out against some left-handers and letting him get acclimated to the majors. The next year was a struggle, and he batted only .233. But as I said before, Al is a special person. He is very determined and knows how to handle adversity. By 1977 he had gotten back to the point where he was hitting .300 against right-handed and left-handed pitchers.

A manager has to help players realize that adjustments are

needed. A manager also has to recognize his players' weaknesses and work around them.

Sometimes that's not easy.

For example, you can't worry about what is on the mind of the player who is being pinch-hit for. What a manager must concern himself with is winning. If you don't make the move and pinch-hit, what are the other twenty-four players going to think? If you pinch-hit, the one guy is upset. If you don't pinch-hit, many of the other players, who know what should be done, are upset.

When some guys come back to the bench after a move, they may give you a dirty look or slam a bat into the rack. If the situation is extreme, the guy will slam the bat in the rack and then *you* will slam a bat into the rack. Or maybe each of you will throw a helmet down the dugout runway. Rick Dempsey and I had an incident in which we both threw some equipment around. These things happen. People are human, and sometimes tempers flare.

After each confrontation I've had, I could go back and say that I could have handled it differently. But each time you learn something and get better at dealing with these things. It's a tough way to learn, but that's life as a manager.

If you have to send someone else up to the plate to get a hit, there isn't any way to get around it. I try to give the player as much warning as possible. Sometimes I may want my starting player to go out to the on-deck circle, even though I plan to pinch-hit for him. As Rick Dempsey walks by, I might tell him that Terry Crowley will probably bat for him. A lot of guys don't understand why they have to go out to the on-deck circle and then get called back to the dugout when you knew they weren't going to hit. Well, first of all, the hitter at the plate might hit a homer and give us the lead, so I'd have no reason to go ahead with the pinch hitter. Or maybe I don't want the opposition to know I'm going to send a left-handed hitter up to the plate until I have to. Why give the other team time to warm up their left-handed reliever? The other manager may not have both a right-hander *and* a left-hander warming up. Say the other manager is a little slow in doing his homework and isn't aware of everyone on your bench—why tip your hand? It's like playing poker and showing your cards to your opponent before making your play: it isn't sound tactics.

Players often got mad at my words. They'd get upset if I hollered at them or even if I said something to them in a nice, quiet tone. They didn't appreciate the message.

There was an episode with Doug DeCinces in 1978 when the Orioles were facing Cleveland in the first game of a doubleheader. DeCinces was playing second base, and there were runners on first and second with one out. A ground ball was hit, and Mark Belanger had to range far to make the play. He caught it and threw to DeCinces at second for the force. The throw was to the outfield side of second, and Doug held on to the ball for quite a while. What Doug didn't notice was that Buddy Bell kept running and scored all the way from second base.

We had a whole infield who could have yelled for Doug to throw home. Someone else could have hollered, but Doug was the one with the ball. When the inning was finally over and the players returned to the dugout, I said, "Hey, that ain't baseball. Wake up out there."

Doug took this personally and answered back. And when he said something, I had to say something. When a player speaks up like that, a manager can say, "Shut your mouth," or "We'll talk about it later." If the player quiets down, the matter can be discussed in the manager's office. But if the player keeps talking, I feel the manager and player should have it out on the spot, speak their minds, and resolve the situation.

Usually I believe a manager should get a player out of the lineup for that particular game, because this type of thing will bother a club. But I don't believe in grudges. They're stupid and nothing good comes from them. I took DeCinces out of the first game of that doubleheader, but he was back in the lineup for the second game.

I realize that people have feelings, and I don't enjoy hurting people's feelings when I have to take them out of a game. But just because a guy is bothered when he's lifted for a pinch hitter, it doesn't necessarily mean he's sensitive. When there are twenty-four players who think the manager should pinch-hit and one player who thinks the manager shouldn't, that one player is not looking at it realistically. A guy may be oh-for-twenty-two and his teammates may be saying, "Boy, this guy is killing us," yet he's angry when the manager benches him. Now, is that being more sensitive or less intelligent?

Ideally, if I didn't have to say one word in the dugout to my players from opening day to the end of the World Series, then it meant we all did our jobs. That is the most healthy situation you can have. Anytime a manager has someone knocking at his door or has to call someone into his office, something is out of kilter. A manager tries to get to the root of a delicate situation as quickly as possible. If there is a problem, it should be discussed face-to-face between the manager and the player, with both parties being honest, not only with each other but with themselves as well. I have asked a player if he truly believes that his ability to catch a fly ball is better than the guy playing ahead of him. Or if he believes that he hits as well as the guy starting at his position. These are tough questions, and they must be answered honestly.

As a manager, I always had rules, so if a guy stepped out of line too often I could say, "Yeah, you broke the rules." When something went wrong, I would tell the press that someone had broken a rule and that I would deal with it—in my own way. That was all I'd say. There was no need for further explanation, because this was strictly between the player and me. Or maybe between the general manager, the player, and me. But that's as far as it should go.

In seventeen years of managing the Orioles, I don't believe I issued more than a few fines. Two were against Earl Williams, because he wouldn't come to the park. There was one occasion when Curt Motton and Elrod Hendricks came to the park ten minutes late for the third time. Then I said they had to kick in twenty-five dollars to the kangaroo court we used to have. I had to do something, because the other players holler when a guy is late a lot.

But if I couldn't sit down with Elrod Hendricks or Curt Motton and talk to them, something was wrong. Anyone who has a player on his team who must be fined before he plays ball doesn't have a very good player. He isn't a very good player if he doesn't want to come to the park or if he doesn't want to play the game right or follow instructions. And if the player is simply incapable, what good does it do to fine him? If he misses signs, what good does it do to keep fining him? What you try to do is figure out a system so

CLUBHOUSE MEETINGS: A REAL WASTE OF TIME

For the most part clubhouse meetings are worthless. I think there should be as few as possible. If you have too many, people don't pay attention and nothing is accomplished. The four or five times a year that a meeting is necessary, I believe in sticking to one subject. When meetings are rare, players usually get the idea that it must be something important.

One reason for calling a meeting might be lack of hustle by the ballclub in general or by some players in particular. A manager can't let something like that slip by, or it will only get worse. When guys begin to jog to first base, something must be done.

Another reason might be if a manager has problems with a player who questions his authority. Sometimes you have to call a meeting to remind the players that you're in charge and that certain conduct won't be tolerated. I would tell the players that I was boss and that I was going to be boss and that that was the way it stood. They had no choice but to accept it.

Another factor might be something like a nine-game losing streak. Then I would usually tell the players to relax and not try to end this thing by themselves. "One guy can't do it alone," I'd tell them. "The talent is here, and I sincerely believe that. The reason you're on my club is that I selected you and I believed you could do a good job. If I didn't think so, you wouldn't be in this clubhouse. If anyone around here is going to leave, I'll probably be the one. I'll make the decisions, you guys worry about your jobs, and we'll be all right. Just be patient. You may not get a hit in your first three trips to the plate, but you could get the hit the fourth time to win the game. Don't give up or get down." This is sort of the opposite of a "let the players know who's boss" meeting. By the end of a 162-game season, a manager probably will have had both kinds of meetings.

One thing is certain—you shouldn't call any meetings when you've won nine in a row: the players are doing just fine without your words. If it's not broke, why try to fix it?

he won't miss the signs. The object is not to take his money but to get him to see the signs.

Sometimes there is a flagrant incident in which a batter stares at the third-base coach, sees the take sign, and then swings away. I've had that happen. When it does, I've used words, sometimes strong words, to let the player know that what he was doing was detrimental to me, to himself, and to the ballclub. In 1969 Don Buford wanted to steal on his own. He took off from first base four times without the sign. I had to make him go sit in the clubhouse and watch the rest of us play for a while.

The power the manager has over a player is that the manager makes out the lineup. The manager decides who plays and who doesn't. Not playing a regular is the biggest fine you can level against him. Players have to get into the lineup to make money. They're in the game because they want to play. The worst thing a player can hear is that he is out of the lineup. And if you run into a guy who signed a five-year, five-million-dollar contract and he says he doesn't care if he plays or not, you may as well pay him off and forget him. You don't win with that type of player.

A manager has to realize that baseball is a game of ups and downs and that people have emotions. But it's disturbing when a player makes an out, comes back to the dugout, and kicks the water cooler or slams some equipment. I believe it bothers the manager, the coaches, and the other players. Nothing can be done right at the moment, unless the case is extreme. Most players go down into the dugout runway and out of sight to vent their frustrations. It's rare that they do it in front of everyone. But when it does happen, it should be discussed after the game, if possible. It doesn't do a bit of good to break helmets or kick drinking fountains or any of that stuff. You see more of this type of behavior in the minors, maybe because outbursts like this can keep players out of the big leagues. They're letting their temper get the better of them, losing control, and being too upset to do their job correctly.

There will always be the pitcher who is mad at himself for throwing a bad pitch, and he may be mad at the manager or his teammates. There will always be a guy who goes into the clubhouse and lets a chair fly. The incident ends up in the newspapers, and property is destroyed. This will always be a part of baseball. People playing checkers will sometimes knock over the board when they lose. But that doesn't make it right. In most instances, the manager can talk to the player and try to get him to show more self-control. Once in a great while there will be a case where a guy goes sort of berserk for a moment and needs to be grabbed so he doesn't hurt himself or someone else. Then there is real trouble.

Breaking things doesn't make a player appear as though he cares more about winning or losing than the guy who is steady. I always told young players to keep cool. The good player knows he will get a hit the next time. The good pitcher knows if he hung that curve and made a mistake to a certain hitter, he won't do it again. It's a feeling of confidence.

Brooks and Frank Robinson never made a scene when they popped up with the bases loaded. Both *knew* they were going to get a hit the next time. Frank's anger was vented at the guy on the mound. If the pitcher made Frank look bad and got him out, Frank would set his mind to hitting the ball out of the park in his next at bat, not ripping up the clubhouse. Or if a guy made a great catch on Frank, he'd tell himself he would hit a ball so far that no one would be able to catch it. This doesn't mean Brooks and Frank weren't disappointed or frustrated when they made outs. It really bothered them, but they knew they would succeed at the next opportunity.

I respect people who have this type of self-control, but I don't hold anything against people who lose their tempers. A manager must accept each player's shortcomings as well as his talents. You cannot ask a player to do something beyond his ability. As a player, I would throw a helmet once in a while. It probably was a result of immaturity. What good does it do to throw a helmet, just because you hit the ball hard and it was caught? Is that going to help you get a hit next time? It makes no sense, and your teammates don't respect you. It's like the guy who throws the club on the golf course because he missed the putt. No one is impressed.

A pitcher can't control the ball and a hitter can't control the bat if they can't control themselves. A lot of these outbursts are eliminated as players age and make their way through the minors. A temper is something that most players can learn to control.

Winning and Losing Players: Baseball's Myth

Sportswriters and announcers spend too much time talking about "clutch" players, "winning" players, and "losing" players. It's true that some players deliver more than other players in crucial situations. It's also true that some players play on more winning teams than others. But you must remember that baseball is a team game. That may be a cliché, but it's also a fact.

No one has hit more home runs than Hank Aaron. He is unquestionably one of the greatest players in the history of the game. But he was with only two teams that made the World Series. Certainly Aaron performed well enough to get to the World Series more than two of the twenty-three years he spent in the majors, but his supporting cast wasn't strong enough to get to the top.

A winning player is nothing more than a player on a winning team. A losing player is a guy who played on a losing team that year. Often the same player goes from being a winning player to being a losing player and then back to being a winning player—all depending on if he's traded and how his club performs. Baseball is so elementary, and people want to make it so complicated. Teams with the most ability will wind up as winners. Those without the talent will get beaten.

In 1982, Dave Winfield had an outstanding season even though his New York Yankees didn't win. He hit the homers, drove in the runs, and played well in the field for the entire season. The man hit 37 homers and threw out guys from left field. That's a winning player, and I don't care if his team finished in first place or last place. *There is no such thing as a "winning" player or a "losing" player.* It comes down to a player's ability and how he produces in any one season. If Winfield had hit .230 with eight homers, you couldn't say he contributed much to winning. But when you consider the year he had in 1982, he would have helped any team in either league to win. Another good player is Toby Harrah. He's had some impressive seasons with Texas and Cleveland, but he hasn't been on a winner. It isn't Harrah's fault, and you can't call him a losing player just because he hasn't been surrounded by enough talent. A guy like Toby Harrah does a lot to help a team win: he steals bases, hits for power, scores a hundred runs a year, and plays every day.

There aren't losing players, there are only players with bad statistics. At the end of the season you try to improve your team by taking the players with bad stats and seeing if you can get someone who will do better in those positions. For years Ken Singleton helped the Orioles win countless games. He was great, and it's impossible to count all the big hits he got for us. But in 1982 his year was not as good as some of his previous ones. He contributed to Baltimore's ninety-five wins, but in the past he had contributed much more. Did he suddenly become a "loser"? And when he bounced back in 1983, did he become a "winner" again? These labels get to be so foolish.

Ernie Banks was probably one of the best players ever, and he did it at two positions—shortstop and first base. But he was with the Cubs for his whole career and didn't have much talent around him. Ernie never made it to a World Series, but who could say it was his fault? If the Cubs had had nine Ernie Banks, or even five, they would have won.

Playing on a winning team helps a player's performance, but perhaps not in the way most people believe. If a team is going well, they usually have a runner on first base. That opens up a hole in the infield and gives hitters a better opportunity to raise their batting averages and drive in runs. It puts the pitcher under pressure. The more guys on base, the more pressure on the defense. The infield has to move in a few steps to play for the double play or the play at home plate. All of this gives the hitter an edge. He has more space for his grounder to make it through the infield. The man still has to get the hit, but the odds have increased in his favor. Put that same guy on a team that's losing, and he'll keep coming up to the plate with the bases empty and his stats won't be as good.

That brings us to Reggie Jackson, considered perhaps the greatest "winning" player of the last twenty years.

I respect Reggie Jackson, and I liked having him play for me in 1976. Reggie has a lot of ability, but he didn't display it from May 2 until the All-Star break because of his contract situation. He went to spring training for about five days and then went back home until May 2, sitting out. Then his "spring training" lasted from May 2 to June 15, which was part of the regular season for the Orioles. We had extra batting practice for him before games and after games. Even after night games there was more batting practice, and we kept the lights on for Reggie so he could get his extra work.

We needed to get Reggie in gear so he could help us win. In that first month he didn't hit much. But a manager can't platoon Reggie. He needed to play, to get his at bats and regain his timing. He had to play the season. Right before the All-Star game, Reggie took off and became the best player in the league during the second half. I enjoyed having Reggie Jackson the same as having any other player. There is one thing I like to do, and that is to treat Tim Nordbrook or Tom Shopay or anyone else the same as Reggie Jackson or any other star. There is individual consideration when a player has a personal problem, but as far as team rules go, everyone is the same.

Reggie has had an amazing career. He has played for some pretty good teams, but he has also played a large part in getting his clubs into the World Series. He has had a lot of opportunities to rise to the occasion, and he has rarely failed to come through. Any manager would love to have someone like him.

When a ballplayer joins a successful team and plays next to someone like Reggie Jackson or Eddie Murray, it's bound to help his performance. The player who has spent some time with a loser and then joins the Orioles knows he is going to play for a good club. The Orioles were going to win quite a few games anyway, even if they didn't have this new player. But most new players know the Orioles are going to win, and they are very willing to contribute. A pitcher coming from a last-place club to the Orioles will have an opportunity to win more games, because Baltimore will score more runs and make better plays than his old club.

When you get to the bottom of most players, you find men who want to win. There is no question that winning is their first concern. Certainly they want to have a good season with excellent statistics, but the biggest satisfaction most players have derives, I believe, from contributing to a championship club.

It's hard to determine if a guy is a clutch player. But I've noticed that some players are tougher in the clutch than others. Even more significantly some players do better in crucial situations against certain teams than they do against other clubs. Some players wear you out and don't hit that much against the rest of the league. When he played for Cleveland, John Lowenstein was an

THE NECKTIE EPISODE

When I managed the Orioles, they had a dress code. I didn't like to wear a coat and tie on a commercial flight when we were going to a warm place like California, but it was club policy and I enforced it. I'm not much on dress codes. I think it's nice to wear a sport jacket when you're in a hotel lobby, but not in Texas when the temperature is 106 degrees.

The Orioles felt that a high-class organization wears ties on the road. I worked for the Orioles, and I did what I was told; I wasn't going to quit my job because I had to wear a tie. Our owner believed in having his employees wear coats and ties, and he was paying everyone good money, even before free agency.

Right after Reggie Jackson joined the Orioles in 1976, he wanted to be the hero of the team and refused to wear a tie on a flight. I told Reggie he couldn't fly with us unless he wore one. He went to the terminal, bought one, and put it on. Reggie was trying to be the hero, but he meant no harm. Once Reggie saw that his refusal to wear a tie could cause some trouble, he stopped it. Frankly, I wish Reggie had won, because then *I* could have skipped the tie when I wanted to. But I had to support my boss. Besides, when you lie in bed and think how thankful you are to be in baseball and making a good living, who cares if you have to wear a tie? If that's what the owner wants, why worry about it?

excellent clutch hitter against the Orioles. Cliff Johnson also used to hurt us. Naturally, a .300 hitter should have more game-winning hits than a .250 hitter. After all, the .300 hitter gets more hits than the guy at .250. But there is no set formula to explain why some players fare better in the clutch than others.

One theory might be that pitchers tend to go to their breaking ball when the game is on the line. This would give hitters who handle the curve pretty well an advantage. Or maybe the player who steps to home plate looking for the breaking ball has a better chance than the normal player.

While power hitters usually have more game-winning RBIs than anyone else, it's a different type of hitter who does the best when it comes to driving in a runner from third base with less than two outs. This situation favors the hitter with a short stroke who makes contact. In 1969 Don Buford drove in seventeen or nineteen runners in that situation. He could get the bat on the ball.

A lot of games are won in the last three innings, and Brooks and Frank Robinson were two of the best hitters I've ever seen from the seventh inning on. But they were good hitters any time. On the whole, I'd say a good clutch player is usually a good player to begin with.

A "WE" TEAM

Shortly after coming to the Orioles, Steve Stone said Baltimore was a "we" team as opposed to an "I" team. By that he meant the Oriole players tended to think in terms of the club as a whole rather than only about themselves. I believe Steve had something in this observation.

I stand by my belief that individual performances are the most important part of baseball. Give me nine guys building good statistics, and I'll show you a good club. But on the Orioles there was a mood in the clubhouse that was free of jealousy and animosity and full of the desire to win a championship. I don't know if it makes a difference on the field, but it does make for a happy atmosphere in the dressing room, on the plane, in the hotel lobby, and everywhere that the team is together.

Maybe the "we" team attitude came about because the Oriole players knew they might be pinch-hit for at any time and any place. What a manager likes to see is the hitter who is taken out of the game cheering for the man replacing him. I remember the first time I had to pinch-hit for Lee May. Earlier in the game I had sent someone in to bat for Rick Dempsey, and we called a catcher out of the bullpen to take his place in the field. That left us with no catchers.

Now Lee May was about to go on deck. Lee had had a great career, hitting twenty-five or thirty homers and driving in around a hundred runs for me season after season. I had never pinch-hit for him before. I said, "Lee, if the guy at the plate gets on, we have to pinch-hit for you." Lee nodded and went out into the one-deck circle. The batter reached first, and that brought up May. I made the move, and it was tough. At the same time we needed a catcher in the bullpen to warm up the pitcher. Dempsey had been playing on a bad leg, and he started to limp toward the bullpen. But Lee stopped Rick and said he would warm up the pitcher. He grabbed the catcher's mitt and went to the bullpen.

That's what it's like on a "we" team. Lee May probably had never warmed up a pitcher in the bullpen before, but he volunteered to do it. He didn't sulk because he was pinch-hit for, even though it had to hurt. The other players saw this gesture, and they knew Lee was dedicated to what was best for the club. Instead of slamming the bat and getting mad at the manager, he helped out in the bullpen. Lee didn't want Dempsey to risk getting hurt even more in the bullpen. He was thinking of others first. You can't ask more of a player than that.

COACHES

The Baltimore Farm System for
Big-League Managers

PERHAPS the best way for someone to become a major-league manager is to coach for the Baltimore Orioles. Jim Frey, Billy Hunter, Frank Robinson, and George Bamberger all coached under me and then became big-league managers. The Orioles have always had some of the best minds in baseball. The highest paid coach in baseball, Charlie Lau of the Chicago White Sox, is a former Oriole coach. While the Orioles' current manager, Joe Altobelli, never coached under me, he did manage Baltimore's Class AAA Rochester farm club. Some believe that Oriole pitching coach Ray Miller is destined to manage in the majors.

A lot of credit has to go to the Baltimore Orioles organization. They attract good people and give them the proper training. And the whole organization, from the low minors to the big club, uses the same system of plays and practice. That gives the organization a valuable asset—continuity.

The first thing a manager looks for in a coach is a man who is not afraid of physical work. One of a coach's main jobs is to throw batting practice. Few people realize it, but a coach who can give you a good batting practice can be worth a lot. Batting-practice pitches usually should be fastballs over the plate. You want the hitters to have something good to swing at, because this helps them with their timing. It doesn't do the hitters any good if the guy on the mound is eating them up with curves and sliders. The purpose of batting practice is for the hitter to get his stance right and his swing right and generally to feel comfortable with his stride as he swings.

Sometimes a coach will throw curves in batting practice, but the hitter is usually warned. The object is to get the hitter ready for the game, but you don't need exact game conditions. Basically the hitters should get as many strikes and as many swings as possible. If a hitter is having trouble with the curve, seeing one curve after another from a coach can help him adjust. Batting practice is 100 percent different than a game, however. Some guys can look so good in batting practice and then look terrible in the game. Eddie Murray is not a good batting-practice hitter, but watch out for him once they play the national anthem!

Coaches often throw thirty minutes or more of batting practice a day, and that's a demanding job. When a coach comes to the park he works, hitting fungoes to the outfield, hitting fungoes to the infield, throwing batting practice, and sometimes warming up pitchers.

A manager should have the right to pick his own coaches, in conjunction with the organization. Sometimes salaries will have a bearing on it, and a manager has to understand that a coach he wants may be too expensive for the front office. That's just an economic reality. But the manager and the organization should try to get the best coaches possible: the best brains, and those young enough to give you a lot of physical work. That will even save some money, since a team might otherwise have to pay $25,000 a year for a batting practice pitcher.

Before I came to the Baltimore Orioles during the winter of 1967–68, the front office was dissatisfied with the coaching staff. Now I don't know if this came from what was said in the papers or by the players, but the front office was not pleased with Hank Bauer's coaching staff. This is nothing against them, because this same coaching staff was with the Orioles when they won the 1966 World Series, but the organization felt there was some trouble. They thought there was too much fooling around in the bullpen and a general breakdown of discipline overall. Sherm Lollar, the bullpen coach, was a great guy and knowledgeable baseball man, but maybe he had become too close to the players. Also, the pitching staff wound up with several sore arms. Harry Brecheen was the pitching coach, and he had had some success under Paul Richards in the early 1960s and naturally did very well with the 1966 World Championship club. However, there was concern about the sore arms and particularly about the young pitchers like Wally Bunker and Jim Palmer, and the organization felt there was something wrong. Another coach, Gene Woodling, had had some personality conflicts with the ballplayers.

After the 1967 season Harry Dalton asked me what we should do. I was the manager at Rochester at the time. Harry said he was dissatisfied with the coaching staff and asked me to recommend someone.

I started with George Staller. He had given me a ton of advice when I was a minor-league manager, and he had been a part of the Orioles organization for a long time. George couldn't pitch batting practice, but I told Harry that I thought Staller would be a fine first-base coach. He got along with everyone and had a knack for cooling people down in stressful situations, which is a wonderful gift. He had the marvelous ability of getting along with the players and of having fun with them, yet of being able to keep their respect and have them listen when he did some teaching.

I also said I'd keep Billy Hunter as the third-base coach. He was a good physical man. He had a great capacity for hard work, and he made a solid first lieutenant for a manager. He could get the players to do their work without alienating them. A manager always needs a first lieutenant-type like Hunter.

Ballplayers will holler at the coaches and give them a lot of crap. That's why a manager must stay 100 percent behind them. A manager tells the players in spring training that words from a coach's mouth are the same as from his mouth.

I mentioned to Harry that if he was unhappy with Brecheen, he had a great pitching coach-teacher in George Bamberger, who had served as our minor-league pitching instructor for a long time. George and I had been together in the minors, and I knew how effective he could be.

As for the bullpen coach, I told Harry that if he wanted someone to sit on people in the bullpen, a mean son of a gun, he should get Vern Hoscheit. He might make some enemies, but he would let the manager know what was going on in the bullpen. To do his job right, Vern needed a manager squarely behind him, or the players would give him a lot of baloney. Vern was a guy who wasn't afraid to do this tough role, and he'd holler at anyone if there was a reason.

Harry Dalton hired all the people I recommended but George Staller. Instead, *I* was named the first-base coach.

In 1968 we started off very poorly. Hank Bauer had won the pennant in 1966 with certain ballplayers, and he felt he had to stick with them. But we had added two players I thought could help the 1968 Orioles: Donny Buford and Elrod Hendricks. Hank didn't think much of them. I'd say Hank had too much loyalty to the players who had done it for him a couple of years before. That's a trap some managers fall into, and it can cost them their jobs. A manager keeps thinking that this guy did it for him so many times before and that he can do it again. But in the case of Bauer, it had been a year and a half since these players had helped him.

In 1972 some people said I stayed with Don Buford too long. He started slowly that year and never did come around. But I didn't play him while he was hitting .200 just out of blind loyalty. My stats showed he had handled certain pitchers very well. I had memories of Donny getting key hits off the same pitchers. After a game in which Buford went oh for four, I'd go home saying he wasn't going to play again. But then the next day I'd be at the park looking at my stats, and I'd realize he was my best hitter against a certain pitcher. Logic, not loyalty or my heart, got Buford back into the lineup. But for once my stats were lying to me. It wasn't Donny's year.

So I can empathize with Hank Bauer in 1968. A manager has to count on certain key players bouncing back. A player who has a bad first half can have a strong second half. It happens to some players every year. You must give veterans a good, honest shot.

I would agonize over this. It's hard to know for sure if a guy is in a slump or if he simply can't do it anymore. A manager is a human being, and he feels things. But when you need to keep your job and put money in your pockets, it isn't quite as hard to take someone out of the lineup as it would be if you were financially secure and didn't need to work. There's an element of complacency. By not making a move, a manager is trying to avoid a tough situation. But a manager can't afford to refuse to make that gut-churning decision. Someone has to be bounced, someone has to be hollered at.

The Orioles have promoted their coaches through the minor-league system. It's a solid mode of operation, but not the only way to do it. As a manager, I had longevity. I had worked with the people in our organization in the past and in spring training. They knew how I wanted things done. No instruction was needed for the coaches promoted from within the organization, because everybody had been using the same methods.

On my last coaching staff, I had Cal Ripken, who had played for me in 1960 and had been in the Orioles organization for twenty-five years. He replaced Hunter, who was hired to manage Texas. When George Staller retired, I went to another Oriole minor-league manager, Jim Frey. When George Bamberger was hired to manage Milwaukee, Ray Miller became the pitching coach. Ray had been our minor-league pitching instructor for five years. When Frank Robinson coached for me, he had the background of having played for the Orioles and had even managed our Rochester farm club, in 1978. I made Elrod Hendricks our bullpen coach because he was a good worker and had spent almost all of his playing career with Baltimore.

I used my coaches for many purposes. When a ballplayer was upset and didn't want to talk to me, I could have a coach talk to him for me. The coach wouldn't make up for me to the player; rather he would tell the player what he needed to be told. He'd give instructions. If it got bad, I'd call the player into my office and take care of it myself.

Sometimes I'd use a coach to give a player the kind of encouragement that he might need but that I don't think should come from the manager. As I said, I don't go in much for a manager patting fannies. But there's no reason you can't use a coach to do it. There was a game in which Sammy Stewart came on in relief and pitched six scoreless innings. He left in the ninth with the score tied. For all his great work, Stewart ended up with nothing—no win, no save. I told Ray Miller to go talk to him and pick up his spirits. If Elrod Hendricks or Cal Ripken was close to someone I had to pinch-hit for, I'd ask him to make sure the player didn't get his nose out of joint. That's a part of managing, just like making out the lineup.

To a certain extent a coach has to be a snitch. Anything he can't handle, or anything that he knows about players getting out of line, he must tell the manager. If the coach doesn't tell the manager, he isn't doing his job. The coaches are around the players a hell of a lot more than the manager, and that enables them to see and sense things. They have to let the manager know what's going on, especially when a player is pissed off at the manager. Maybe the manager upset a player and doesn't realize that it happened. That shouldn't be a regular occurrence, but it will happen. If a coach hears a player badmouthing, he must report it to the manager. Then the manager can call the player into the office, go face-to-face with him, and clear the air. It's the only way to get these things straightened out. You can't let problems fester.

Often a coach doesn't have to report the bad words—they show up in the morning paper the following day. I've never criticized a ballplayer for saying anything to the press, but that player should tell me what's on his mind, too.

Of course, the main attributes of a coach are intelligence and the ability to teach. That's where their real value lies. Knowledge of the game and the players means a lot.

The First-Base Coach

During the game the first-base coach's job is to watch the first baseman. He has to be aware of where the first baseman is playing when there's a runner on. Is he back? Is he holding the runner on? Is he sneaking in behind the runner? The coach should constantly remind the runner of the number of outs and tell him to be sure to break up the double play. The coach also must be aware so he can yell a warning if the pitcher makes a pickoff move to first. He should tell the runner the situation, tell him to tag up or take off, remind him to go to third on a single to right. When there are runners on first and second and the first baseman is playing behind the runner, the coach shouldn't watch the hitter; he should keep his eye on the first baseman so he can tell the runner if the fielder is coming in behind him for a pickoff attempt.

The Third-Base Coach

The third-base coach has to make fast decisions while a play is in progress. He has to make decisions on a ball hit behind the runner. For example, say there's a runner on first and the batter hits a single to right field. The runner will go hard to second and round the bag and should pick up the third-base coach at this point. Since the runner can't see the play, it's up to the coach to hold him at second or wave him to third. The same principle holds true with a runner on second on a base hit to the outfield. When that runner goes to third, he should watch the coach to find out if he should try to score or stop at third. There are some players who don't need a coach on the bases. Brooks and Frank Robinson always seemed to know if they should go from first to third on a single to right or if they could score from second on a base hit. Eddie Murray has the same ability. It's a matter of intelligence and instincts with these guys. They simply know what to do. Other runners need the help of a coach.

A player should follow a coach's directions on the bases. The coach usually has a better view as well as a good knowledge of the outfielder's arm. A third-base coach must have excellent instincts, too. He has to make up his mind almost in an instant whether to send the runner or hold him up. In a close game that's a crucial decision. A manager needs talented coaches he can trust.

Some outfielders fool runners. The Oakland outfield of Tony Armas, Rickey Henderson, and Dwayne Murphy got to the ball as quickly as any three outfielders I have seen. A runner should be wary in these situations. Henderson is one of the most amazing guys I have ever seen. He gets to the ball in a second, and he can throw extremely well. A runner has to be careful when a ball is hit to him. Bobby Bonds would get to the ball extremely quickly, but he made a lot of poor throws. A runner has to know if there is a Henderson or a Bonds in the outfield. Naturally, so does a coach.

A manager will give signals to the third-base coach. Those signs are different from the ones the coach relays to the hitters. I kept my signs to the third-base coach very simple.

If the standard signs are too complicated for certain players, a good third-base coach will work out some individual signs with the people in question. The key part about signs is having a set the ballplayers can understand but that won't be stolen by the opposition. There is very little stealing of signs in the majors. However, when Frank Robinson was playing, he would pick up the steal sign from Ralph Houk. Frank got it when he was playing right field because he had the angle, a perfect view of Houk in the dugout. When Frank got the steal sign, he'd give a sign of his own to the catcher. We'd call a pitchout and get the runner. This was in Yankee Stadium, where Houk would be on the top step of the dugout, tossing pebbles. Most managers stay back in the dugout when they give their signs, out of sight of half the field.

STEALING SIGNS

When signs are stolen, they're being sent either from the manager to the third-base coach or from the third-base coach to the hitter. Both are difficult to pick off. But even when you do steal signs, you don't have them for very long. Say you find out that a runner is stealing on a 2–2 pitch. The manager calls for the pitchout, and the runner is nabbed. Well, the guy in the other dugout isn't stupid. He'll see what happened and immediately change his signs. Stealing the steal sign might work once all year. You might get more mileage from the bunt sign, because in most situations the bunt is so obvious that no one is sure if you stole the sign or were simply guessing that there'd be a bunt. Usually you know the opposition has your bunt sign if it's clearly a bunt situation but you let your hitter swing away—and on the pitch the infielders don't move. That indicates the other team has your sign because they knew the bunt *wasn't* on. Over the course of the season, you'll have to change your signs maybe three or four times, either because you think they've been stolen or because you've traded someone who naturally knows them.

Some players never learn to get signs. That's a real problem. A manager must then weigh the player's capabilities against his incapabilities. If a player will hurt you more than he helps you, you get rid of him. If his talent is overwhelming, then you have to accept that liability. But that doesn't mean you stop searching for a set of signs he can handle. Very, very few great players have trouble with signs. Some people who are traded a lot have trouble with signs.

It all starts in Little League, maybe in high school. At that level the kids learn how to look for signs and how to discern them. If they don't get used to doing that when they are very young, they have one hell of a time with it when they are pros. If the players ignore signs in Little League, they aren't apt to catch them in high school or anywhere else until someone sits on them or until they've lost a baseball job. Then they have to look in the mirror and find out why they were cut, and if they had trouble with signs, they should ask themselves if that was the reason.

I'm not talking about one guy missing one sign. That will happen once in a while. But when there's a pattern, a consistency in failing to get the signs, you have a problem.

The Pitching Coach

The Orioles have had only three pitching coaches in their history: Harry Brecheen, George Bamberger, and Ray Miller. When I talk about continuity, this is a great example.

I feel I know quite a bit about pitching. It's a manager's decision when to take out a pitcher, who to bring in, and how to set up a staff. A manager naturally listens to all the information he can get, especially from the pitching coach, but in the end, it's his decision.

However, the pitching coach has a very important job. OK, though I can't throw a curve, I know what a good one looks like. But knowing the mechanics of a pitcher's motion is a whole different matter. I also may know when a pitcher should use a curve or a slider to help him win. But that doesn't mean I can teach him how to throw one. That's when I would go to the pitching coach and say, "Why don't you work with Torrez on developing a slow curve?" or "Why don't you see if you can teach Flanagan a changeup?" The coach does the actual instruction. He will spend hours with a pitcher in the bullpen, perfecting one thing or seeking to iron out a little flaw.

A pitching coach is also in charge of conditioning the pitchers. That can be the difference between winning the pennant and ending up in second place. There is no way to avoid sore arms, but you want to keep them to a minimum. The same thing goes for muscle pulls and any other kind of injury. A good coach will have his pitchers in shape, especially their legs. He will make sure they do their running before every game.

I often talked to my pitching coach during games. I would send him to the mound when I felt the pitcher needed to be settled down or if I had a specific idea I thought the coach could best communicate. Sometimes a pitching coach will want to go to the mound because he thinks he has spotted something the pitcher is doing wrong. That's great. A manager should send the coach out there. This is a team. Everyone should be pulling together, and any good advice is appreciated. A manager and his coaches should always be working together.

UMPIRES

I've Been Thrown Out of
All the Best Places

I GOT EJECTED from games in Fitzgerald, Georgia, and Boston, Massachusetts. I got tossed from an exhibition game in Fort Myers, Florida, from an Instructional League game in Scottsdale, Arizona, and from a World Series game in New York. I even was tossed once when the Orioles played an exhibition game in Japan.

None of it was ever calculated. I was always just being myself. When I went out to argue with an umpire, I said what was on my mind. I didn't go out there wanting to embarrass anyone. You know the old saying, "Be true to yourself." That was what I did. If the umpires made a mistake, I let them know.

George Steinbrenner once said he thought my handling of umpires was worth eight or ten wins a year, but I don't buy that. All I was doing was being honest. I wasn't trying to get anything from the umpires that shouldn't have been ours in the first place. I tried to be fair with umpires, and I thought they did their best when it came to me.

The main thing I want to say about umpires is that I never had anything against them. I didn't dislike them. They're a part of the game. They make the decisions about who's out and who's safe, what's a strike and what isn't, and basically who's right and who's wrong. The umpires do call things "the way they see 'em," as the old saying goes. But a manager will just see some of the plays differently.

Whether the manager is right or wrong when he goes out to argue a call is irrelevant. The fact is that two people often see things differently, and when that happens, there's going to be a disagreement. Umpires make hundreds of calls a game, especially behind the plate. That means I've actually argued on only a very small percentage of them.

EARL WEAVER'S EJECTIONS, BY UMPIRE

Anthony	1	Haller	6	Palermo	3
Barnett	3	Heitzer*	1	Parks	1
Bremigan	4	Hirschbeck	1	Phillips	1
Brinkman	4	Kaiser	1	Reilly	1
Clark	2	Kunkel	2	Rice	1
Cooney	3	Luciano	7	Roe	3
Crawford	1	Maloney	4	Runge	1
Deegan	1	McCoy	1	Springstead	7
Denkinger	2	Merrill	1	Umont	2
DiMuro	2	Morganweck	1	Valentine	1
Evans	5	Napp	3	Welke	1
Flaherty	1	Neudecker	1	West	1
Ford	3	O'Connor*	1	Young	1
Garcia	4	Odom	3	TOTAL	99
Goetz	3	O'Donnell	3		

* Amateur umpires during strike of 1979.

† Totals include ninety-seven regular-season ejections, one spring-training ejection, and one World Series ejection."

Umpiring is an underpaid profession, and a guy has to give up an awful lot to be an umpire. The pay and expenses of working through the minors doesn't make umpiring profitable. It isn't a job for people who want to get rich. The lack of financial gain, especially at first, stops a lot of good people from entering that line of work, as long as they have the intelligence to do something else. Umpires have to be very dedicated to accept what they make in the minors. There's no doubt that these men love the game. They have to work hard.

To be an ump, a man has to give up his regular job and pay his own way through umpire school, hoping that there might be an opening in the minors once he's finished his training. We all know that big-league umpires don't get fired, so those in the minors have to wait until someone decides to retire. The turnover is not great, which means there are few jobs at the top. Many competent men get stuck in the minors and it's tough to be in the minors year after year while earning almost nothing. If there was a higher wage in the minors, there would be more applicants. The more people there are who apply, the more likely it is that there will be better-quality umpires.

Umpires are paid based on longevity. A second-year umpire earns far less than a ten-year umpire, despite the fact that the second-year umpire may be better than the ten-year man. It isn't the best system, but umpires have always been paid by seniority, so that's the way it is.

Some have said that I can accept inadequacies in my players but not in umpires. That completely misses the point. I can't tolerate anyone's mistakes. When my players made a mistake, I hollered at them. When an umpire made a mistake, I hollered at him. Not every player is a .300 hitter, not every ball is caught, and umpires are bound to miss some calls. But I felt it was my duty to speak up when a mistake was made. It was nothing personal, just a part of my job.

An umpire who misses a call can, and will, beat you in a close game. That's why it's so important for an umpire to do his job right. A bad call will beat the Orioles the same way a ball that managed to go through the legs of Mark Belanger will. Errors on any front hurt and hurt bad. I don't yell at a player for a physical error, for example, the ball going through his legs. But say Rich Dauer misses a sign or doesn't line up in the right place for a cutoff throw—then I'll let him know he messed up. That's the same way I inform the umpires of a mistake. Everyone talks about what sound fundamental baseball the Orioles play. There's no question it gave us an edge, but that edge is only there if the umpires call a tight game. I knew my players didn't make the phantom tag at second, so I wanted to make sure the umps didn't let the other team get away with one. The more by the book they called the game, the better it was for us.

When a manager goes out to talk to an umpire, he can do almost anything he wants. You can't physically abuse an umpire, and I made a point never to curse an umpire. But a manager must do what he feels will make him be understood, say whatever is necessary to get the point across, even if he must resort to something like, "You lost us the ballgame."

THREE BASIC RULES FOR ARGUING WITH UMPIRES

1. **First, never curse an umpire. Curse the call, say it was a bleeping bad call, but never call the umpire a name. Try not to get personal.**
2. **Know the rules. If you know the rules, you might win one now and then. There was a game in Cleveland it seemed we had lost. There was an overthrow with a runner on first base, and the ball went off the playing field. The umpires permitted the runner to score, but I knew the rule book said the runner was supposed to stop at third. I went out to talk about the call, even though the players were in the dressing rooms and it seemed that the game was over. But the umpires realized they had made a mistake on the ruling. They brought both clubs back on the field, and we ended up beating Cleveland that night when most people thought the Indians had defeated us.**
3. **Be yourself when you're dealing with umpires or anyone else in this world. Remember, you can't fool anyone.**

Of course, the umpires won't accept that. They would say things to me like, "You lost the game when you didn't give the bunt sign in the fourth inning." Or "Your center fielder lost the game by striking out four times." Or "Your pitcher lost the game because he can't throw the ball over the plate." You get that one if you are asking about a ball-strike call. "It ain't me that's losing the game," the umpire will say. "Get that player out of the game. It's his fault."

A manager should say whatever is on his mind. There is no way to give specific instructions on how to argue with an umpire. It's up to the individual manager and has a lot to do with a man's personality.

The only way I kept my job for fifteen years was by winning games. It's a tough thing to take when someone you haven't selected to play for your team makes a mistake.

When a player argues with an umpire, the manager must quickly get on the field and say the words the player wants said to the umpire. You can't tell your player to shut up; you have to back him. The player is playing for you, and the manager should never forget that. Like you, his main goal is to win the game. A manager must keep his player in the game, even if he isn't sure the player is right in his claim.

WEAVER'S TENTH LAW

The job of arguing with the umpire belongs to the manager, because it won't hurt the team if he gets thrown out of the game.

In 1982 I let Eddie Murray get thrown out of a game because I didn't react fast enough. Dennis Martinez was pitching for the Orioles and was called for a balk. I thought Dennis had balked, too. But Eddie was arguing with the first-base umpire. I went out with one object in mind: to get Eddie out of the argument and keep him in the game. I said a few words, but I kept pretty calm. I got Eddie away from the umpire and headed back to the dugout. But as Eddie was walking away, he hollered something over his shoulder at the umpire—and was ejected. If I had argued with more enthusiasm, Eddie would have left the scene earlier and probably wouldn't have been run out of the game. Later I saw a replay on television, and Eddie was right. Things like that will cost the game, because a guy like Eddie Murray might go to bat in the eighth or ninth inning with the chance to win it. I don't bat, so it doesn't matter if I get ejected or stay in the dugout. A manager must do whatever he can to keep his players in the game. It really doesn't hurt the team if he's ejected, certainly not in the same way that it does when someone like Eddie Murray is tossed.

Does all that arguing do any real good? Well, there are two schools of thought. It's been written that antagonizing the umpires will hurt a team because it may cost them a close call. Others say that a manager who stays on top of the umpires will get the calls to go his way. Believe either one you want; it had no bearing on the way I managed. I looked at it this way: the next time a close play comes up, the umpire will call it the way he sees it. He might see it right or wrong, it might go in your favor or not. But I always felt that by staying on top of the umpires, I could help make sure they'd stay on top of the play. Sure, it bothers you when a call goes against you. But nothing's worse than when the umps make a *mistake* that goes against you. Those are what I wanted to elimi-nate—the mistakes that go against you.

During a game you sit in the dugout and laugh at calls that go your way. You say you're on a hot roll, that everything is falling into place, even the umpires. Some things happen that leave you saying, "My Lord, how lucky can we be?" But the next one might go against your team, and the next thing you know, you're on a losing streak.

Over my seventeen years I feel that as many calls went my way as went against me. I sincerely believe it evened out, because the umpires were always trying their best.

I believe that my personality had no bearing on the way the umpires called an Orioles game. They were going to call what they were going to call, and I was going to do what I was going to do. Each of us was doing his job the way he saw fit.

A call may hurt you, but it can also win a game for you. Of course, the ones you remember most are the ones that cost you the game. One day the Orioles were playing in Texas. The score was tied with one out in the ninth. Texas loaded the bases. A ball was hit in front of the plate, and our catcher, Elrod Hendricks, caught it on one bounce and stepped on the plate. Jerry Neudecker was the home-plate umpire. He should have called it a force play for the second out, but for some reason he was looking for a tag play at the plate. But Elrod didn't have to tag the base runner. Anyway, the runner slid into the plate after Elrod had stepped on it. Neudecker made the safe sign, the players ran off the field, and the game was over. Then Neudecker didn't know what to do. That's how a call can cost you a game. You can argue from now until the end of the world, but the game is over and you lost. Those calls really hurt.

Some people say that umpires tend to give some players better calls than others. I really believe the umpire calls them the way he sees them, but that doesn't make all of his calls correct. I don't think that Carl Yastrzemski got a different strike zone than a rookie breaking into the league. The worst thing I can say is that an umpire may lose his composure and give the pitcher a few pitches against a certain hitter for one particular at bat. That doesn't happen too often, but umpires are like ballplayers, managers, and everyone else: they can get upset. Suppose a hitter said something in his last at bat that angered the umpire. The umpire just may stretch the point a bit when that hitter comes to bat again. That certainly isn't a regular occurrence, but I have seen it happen.

For this reason a player should let the manager handle the umpires. The player won't benefit from getting mad at the umpire, and he runs the risk of paying for it his next time up. But part of the manager's job is to handle the umpires. Let the umpire get mad at the manager and not the player.

I never felt that umpires were out to get me or anyone else. When I think back on all the one-run games the Orioles won in my fifteen years, I know that umpires gave an honest day's work. Let's face it, one or two bad calls won't make the difference in a 9–2 game. But in those 4–3 and 3–2 games, they can change the outcome. If the umps had been out to get me with their calls, we wouldn't have won so many tight games.

I do know, though, that after a manager has been ejected a number of times, he doesn't receive much leeway when he walks on to the field to discuss a call. I've had umpires say to me, "You ain't going to last long, get off the field," when I had barely said anything. They eject some managers much faster than others. Someone like Dave Garcia, who was rarely ejected as a manager, could say the same thing as me, but the result would be different. I would usually get the thumb, while Dave would be able to stay in the game. There have been games when I started to say something to an umpire but was stopped by him saying, "Get out of here, we heard this before."

One ejection in 1982 was a beauty. Bill Haller was umpiring behind the plate, and he told my catcher to give me a message. Haller said to tell me I couldn't leave the dugout or I'd be ejected. I told my catcher that the next inning I'd be out of the dugout on the second pitch and that he should tell that to Heller. On the second pitch, I stepped out of the dugout and walked straight to the mound to see my pitcher. Haller walked out from behind the plate. He thought I was going to say something to him, but I ignored him and talked to my pitcher, taking my time. Then I turned around and walked away without saying a word to Haller. But I did smile, because I wanted to show him I could go out of the dugout. At that point he threw me out—for smiling, I suppose.

Now, if you ask me that is completely illegal. If we had lost, the game should have been replayed from that point. But there are no criteria for throwing someone out of a game. Umpires have complete freedom in this area; they can throw anyone out for any reason, and there's nothing you can do about it. The bottom line was that Haller didn't want me to come out of the dugout to argue on a play. It bothered him that I would show everyone that I *could* come out of the dugout. It was a joke, but Bill lost his composure and ended up looking foolish. Legally I felt I had a protest, if Lee MacPhail, president of the American League, wanted to uphold it. But we won the game so it became academic.

When I say something to an umpire, it's not because I'm trying to work him over, or because it's part of a grand strategy. I'm objecting to that particular play. Either I feel the umpires made a mistake, or I'm out there to defend my players and say what they want expressed. If all the hitters come back to the dugout and complain that the strike zone is too big, a manager has to holler to the umpire that the strike zone is too large. And if all the players start hollering at the umpires because they feel something's wrong and because they want to win, the manager can't tell his players to shut up. A manager has to stand up for his players. He should get up, in full view of his players, and go say what needs to be said. The manager usually keeps talking to the umpires until the players quiet down. Then, if the umpires get angry at what's been said, the manager receives the brunt of their fury. That way if someone is going to get tossed, it's the manager. The players, who can win the game, will remain on the field.

I'd say I got myself thrown out about half the time. In the other instances, I was doing what I had to for my players.

EARL WEAVER'S EJECTIONS, BY SEASON

1968	(2)	**1974**	(cont.)	**1979**	(9)
7/30	Valentine	9/2	Odom	4/13	Heitzer
9/2	Napp	9/11	Luciano	4/21	O'Connor
				6/18	Barnett
1969	(5)	**1975**	(10)	6/25	Parks
5/13	Runge	5/1	Springstead	7/10	Garcia
6/29	O'Donnell	6/9	Bremigan	8/8	Evans
8/2	Haller	6/14	Brinkman	8/16	Palermo
8/3	Umont	6/28	Luciano	8/18	Palermo
10/15	Crawford	7/8	Evans	8/26	Luciano
		8/15	Luciano		
1970	(3)	8/15	Luciano	**1980**	(5)
7/2	O'Donnell	8/16	Denkinger	3/14	West
7/19	DiMuro	9/6	Maloney	7/6	Roe
9/4	Rice	9/12	Brinkman	8/16	Garcia
				9/10	Palermo
1971	(3)	**1976**	(9)	9/17	Haller
6/6	O'Donnell	4/19	Goetz		
7/20	Napp	4/27	Brinkman	**1981**	(3)
9/6	Barnett	5/25	Luciano	5/18	Merrill
		6/20	Garcia	9/4	Bremigan
1972	(4)	6/28	Evans	9/18	Ford
5/6	Springstead	7/9	Haller		
5/27	Flaherty	7/10	Haller	**1982**	(7)
7/11	DiMuro	7/25	Ford	7/10	Maloney
9/30	Odom	8/24	Deegan	7/16	Cooney
				7/17	Cooney
1973	(8)	**1977**	(7)	8/3	Kaiser
4/15	Evans	5/12	Springstead	8/4	Haller
5/31	Umont	5/25	Brinkman	9/5	Haller
6/29	Maloney	6/23	Maloney	9/30	Roe
7/3	Morganweck	7/23	Bremigan		
7/26	Kunkel	8/16	Clark	**1985**	(4)
8/12	Springstead	8/24	Denkinger	7/22	Ford
9/17	Kunkel	8/25	McCoy	8/11	Hirschbeck
9/29	Luciano			9/29	Evans
		1978	(7)	9/29	Bremigan
1974	(8)	4/23	Reilly		
4/23	Napp	7/5	Springstead	**1986**	(5)
5/4	Barnett	7/6	Springstead	6/10	Roe
5/26	Anthony	7/14	Goetz	6/17	Cooney
6/25	Goetz	7/30	Garcia	8/17	Young
7/12	Springstead	8/5	Neudecker	9/3	Welke
8/9	Odom	8/12	Phillips	9/21	Clark

Corked Bats and Spitballs

Every year there are whispers about certain players. The word is that a hitter who is suddenly having a good year is doing more than swinging a good bat—he's swinging a loaded or corked bat.

They've never done any research on it, but a corked bat is bound to make a player a better hitter. I know, because I used one.

Then there are the pitchers who come into their prime in their late twenties or early thirties. Some of them may have finally learned to control their fastballs or developed a trick pitch such as a knuckleball, but others went from losers to winners thanks to a little help from their medicine cabinets. Some pitchers put Vaseline, hair tonic, or other substances on the ball. Others use saliva. Some cut the ball up with sandpaper or nails.

A good spitball or cutball is one mean pitch. In most cases the hitter can't do much with it besides beat it into the dirt. Batters use corked bats, pitchers doctor the ball. Personally I think too much emphasis is placed on this stuff. If some guys spent as much time improving their game as they do trying to get around the rules, they'd be far better players.

I've managed pitchers who used the spitter, and I've seen some corked bats lying around. You know that Norm Cash used a corked bat when he played for Detroit, because he admitted it. When Norm was questioned about his bat at home plate, he would go back to the dugout and put it away. It's also public record that Graig Nettles and Dan Ford used corked bats, because they were caught using them in games. Ford was playing for California when he hit a pitch and the top of his bat flew off, revealing the cork.

I don't know what an umpire can do to stop the cheating. In 1982 Gaylord Perry was ejected by an umpire for doctoring a baseball. Determining what is a legal pitch and what isn't is a terrible burden to place on an umpire, but someone has to accept the responsibility. An experienced baseball man can recognize a spitter. I can. If I were standing behind home plate, when someone threw a spitter, there would be no doubt in my mind.

But umpires are in a difficult spot. Will the American League hierarchy keep the umpire out of court if he throws a pitcher out of a ball game for cheating? There's always the possibility of a lawsuit these days, and if the umpires are to act decisively, they have to know that the league office is behind him. Everyone's rights must be protected. I don't believe an umpire should eject a pitcher unless he knows he threw a spitter. There are some umpires who can't recognize a spitter, but they wouldn't throw anyone out. If the umpire can recognize a spitter, he should have the power to first warn the pitcher and then eject him if the violation continues. But that isn't enough. There should also be a suspension, forcing the pitcher to miss a couple of starts. In a pennant race that would be the biggest penalty a team could suffer; losing a key pitcher in September even for two starts could mean the difference between first place and second.

If a pitcher can get away with throwing a spitter, and if he can control it, it's a great pitch. But the spitter can get a lot of pitchers in trouble because they can get very wild with it. The pitcher has to squeeze it out of his hand so that it comes to home plate with no spin. It's not an easy pitch to throw. But if a pitcher has a good spitter, it really sinks, maybe a foot or more.

It's interesting that another pitch with no spin is the knuckleball. The knuckleball is legal, yet the spitter isn't. Why? I can't answer that. One of the reasons they made the spitball illegal in the old days was that it was dangerous. Back then hitters didn't wear batting helmets, and too many people were being plunked in the head. It wasn't safe, especially when an inexperienced pitcher was trying to throw it. I think the spitter should be legal for pitchers who know how to use it. It would probably be a good idea to legalize the spitter and to then let the hitters use corked bats.

A corked bat can really help a hitter. I hit six homers in about a month in New Orleans in 1955. Those were the only six I had all year, and they came off a corked bat. When the head of the bat is cut open and filled with cork, it lightens the bat head. That makes it much easier to swing. The effect is like the hard rubber inside a golf ball. That rubber makes the ball carry when it's hit by a club. I can attest to the fact that a baseball carries extremely well when it's hit by a corked bat.

No one's really sure if the corked bat works because it lightens the head or because of the resiliency of the cork. By taking the wood out of the center of the bat, the bat's weight might be reduced to twenty-seven or twenty-eight ounces from thirty-three or thirty-four. Someone ought to try legalizing a hollow bat for spring training. Then we'd find out if the ball travels better simply because the bat is lighter or if the cork is the reason. In spring training one year they used a livelier ball. So why not try hollowed-out bats? Then the question of the importance of a corked bat would be answered.

When you're managing against someone who you believe is using a corked bat, the catcher is sometimes able to spot something on the bat that shows it's been tampered with. Usually it's marked in some way. When he was with California, Dan Ford had pins holding the cork in his bat. That's kind of a lazy way to do it. The smarter way is to drill a hole in the top of the bat, fill it with cork, and then plug the top of it with some plastic wood and sand it. That makes it much harder to detect.

The players hear about who is using a corked bat or who is throwing a spitter. The word gets around. But spitters and corked bats have been a part of the game almost since the beginning. The way things are now doesn't work, because even though these things are illegal a number of people use them. The umpire can't enforce the rules for various reasons.

I never told a player to cheat, and I don't believe it's a good idea to. I'd prefer players who have the talent to hit homers with a regular bat and throw a 90-mile-an-hour fastball. Those are the guys who help you win.

SCOUTING

It's in the
Cards

THE ORIOLES have an index card on every player in the American League. When a player gets traded or sent to the minors, we don't throw out his card; rather, it gets placed in our dead file, from which it can be retrieved if and when he comes back.

I can't really say how much it means in terms of wins and losses to keep accurate and in-depth records on the opposition, but let me put it this way: it never hurts. The more preparation the better. I always kept plenty of records, so I don't know what it would be like to manage without them. I'll say this: I wouldn't want to find out. It's only common sense to want to know everything you can about any obstacle that might be in front of you.

When the Orioles faced a rookie pitcher we had never seen, I sought out information on him. I checked with our advance scout, Jim Russo, and I would see if any of our players had faced him in the minors or perhaps in winter ball. I wanted to get an index card on the guy as soon as possible.

On the cards I wrote any information that I felt was useful. Mostly there are four or five things that give you an idea of a player's strengths, weaknesses, and tendencies.

Every hitter has something different about him. It's pretty safe to say that most like fastballs. Let's face it, it's almost impossible to hit a great breaking pitch that is thrown to the right spot with any authority. Then again, it is very hard for the pitcher to unleash such a pitch.

Minnesota's Kent Hrbek is a fine young hitter. He's very strong and has a lot of intelligence at the plate. Given the choice, he'd like a fastball on every pitch—he's not thrilled by changeups. He's primarily a location hitter; he likes the ball, especially breaking pitches, up. He hits to all fields, so you have to play him straight away and keep the ball down.

Mike Hargrove is a very selective hitter. Unlike Hrbek, he'll take a lot of pitches, and the count always seems to go to 3–2 when he's at the plate. Hargrove will look over a lot of pitches early in the count, so it's crucial that the pitcher get ahead of him. Hargrove is usually waiting for a fastball, which he likes to pull. He gets few hits to left-center field, so you can shade the shortstop in toward second base. Since he's not known as a power hitter, the outfielders don't have to play any deeper than normal.

It's important to know these things. Hrbek looks for a pitch in a certain area (high), while Hargrove waits for a fastball and doesn't worry about its location, so long as it's a strike.

Carlton Fisk differs from these two players in that he's a pull hitter and likes the ball low. He has a very quick bat and is able to pull an outside pitch down the left-field line. For this reason some pitchers will go inside on him. He is also very smart and tends to look for a certain pitch in a certain situation. Most people pitch him inside and play the outfield to pull. A pitch in the right spot can force Fisk to break his bat.

As you can see from the cards, the best pitch against Reggie Jackson is a high inside fastball. Do not give him an inside breaking pitch. Keep the slow stuff outside. You can also use a changeup against him.

The defense against Reggie is interesting. If he hits the ball on the ground, it usually goes up the middle, so the second baseman and shortstop should play him toward the bag. But the outfield has to play him to pull. It isn't enough to just say that so-and-so is a pull hitter. This kind of breakdown is crucial.

On the other hand, Gorman Thomas is a dead pull hitter, both on the ground and in the air. Like Reggie, he has tremendous power and looks for a pitch he can belt into the seats. He has a tendency to chase outside breaking balls. The way to pitch to him is to get ahead in the count and then try to get him to chase a bad breaking ball. Unlike Reggie, Thomas isn't usually a threat to steal a base.

The pitching cards tell the hitter what to look for when he goes to bat. They also show what the pitcher likes to throw when he has

---

Willie Randolph   2B   RH

Excellent high FB hitter

Start with breaking balls and stay with breaking balls

If you have to throw a FB, keep it down

OF—give both lines, average depth

INF—1st and 3rd off the line, 2nd and SS up the middle

Reggie Jackson   OF   LH

Best place for FB is up and in

Keep all breaking balls on the outside half

Can change

OF—LF deep in left-center, CF shade to right, RF straight

INF—SS up the middle, 2B a step toward 2nd

Will steal at times

Gorman Thomas   OF   RH

Best place for FB is up and in

Will guess curve and can hit curve in the strike zone

Slider has to be down and on the outside half, preferably for a ball

Can change

Play to pull all over

two strikes on the batter and what he will use when he is behind in the count.

With Tommy John it's impossible to guess. He's a veteran with great control and can throw any pitch at any time. But he relies on his sinker. The hitter has to lay off the low pitch. John's sinker appears to be right at the knees, but it usually drops low. Nevertheless, most hitters chase it and beat it into the ground. That's why the man is such a great pitcher.

Jack Morris is a power pitcher with a superb slider. When he's behind in the count, he stays with the hard stuff.

These sample pitchers' cards show the kind of notes we keep.

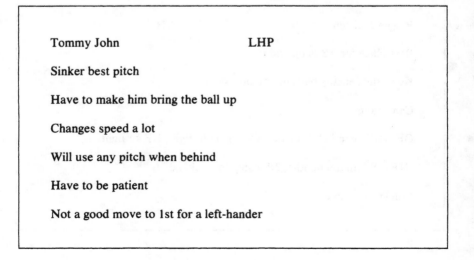

Tommy John   LHP

Sinker best pitch

Have to make him bring the ball up

Changes speed a lot

Will use any pitch when behind

Have to be patient

Not a good move to 1st for a left-hander

Jack Morris   RHP

Good FB—over 90 mph

Excellent slider

Will use curve and change

Mostly FB and slider when behind in count

Fair move to 1st

The Pitching Chart

Every team keeps pitching charts, but each manager has his own system and use for them. The information that comes from these charts is very important.

The chart in this book is of a game between the Orioles and the Cleveland Indians early in the 1983 season. Jim Palmer started the game and left after five innings. Storm Davis and Tippy Martinez finished the game, which was a 2–0 Baltimore victory.

You can tell exactly what happened in this game from looking at the charts. The system for keeping charts is somewhat like that for keeping a scorecard. Each position is given the usual number: the pitcher is 1, the catcher is 2, and so on.

On top of the chart there is a code for the pitches—1 is a fastball, 2 is a curve, etc. Next to each hitter's name is a set of little boxes with "B" and "S" marked beside them. The B boxes are for pitches that were balls, and the S boxes are for pitches that were strikes. The larger box at the bottom left is for the result of the at bat. For example, "F-7" is a fly ball to left field, "K" is a strikeout, and "1B-8" is a single to center field. The little box in the bottom right-hand corner keeps track of the outs in each inning. Finally, the large open area is for notes.

The first hitter in this game was Mike Hargrove. Palmer started him off with a fastball that was a ball. The next pitch is coded "1F"—a fastball that was fouled off. The third pitch is "1S"—a

PITCHING CHART

F - Pitch fouled off
X - HIT - RUN
S - SWING
1 - FAST BALL
2 - CURVE
3 - CHANGE
4 - SLIDER
5 - SCREW BALL
6 - KNUCKLE BALL

Pitcher — Palmer

PAGE: 1

DATE April 15, 1983   WEATHER 51° W15 - blowing in

R H E

Cleveland
AT
Baltimore

PREPARED BY _____

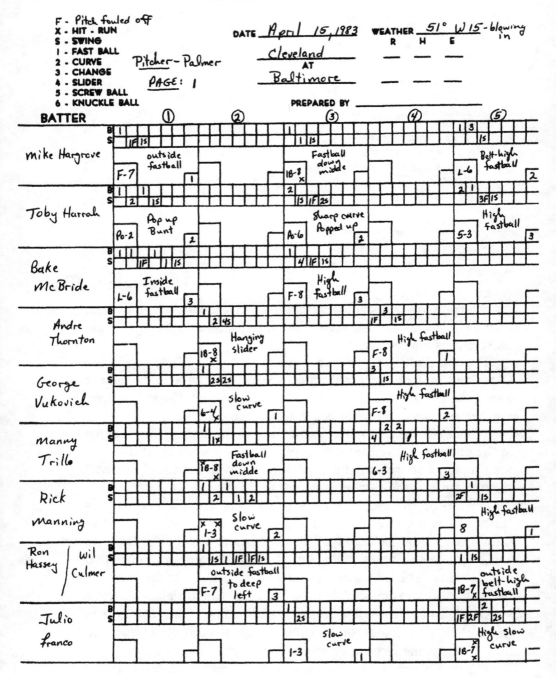

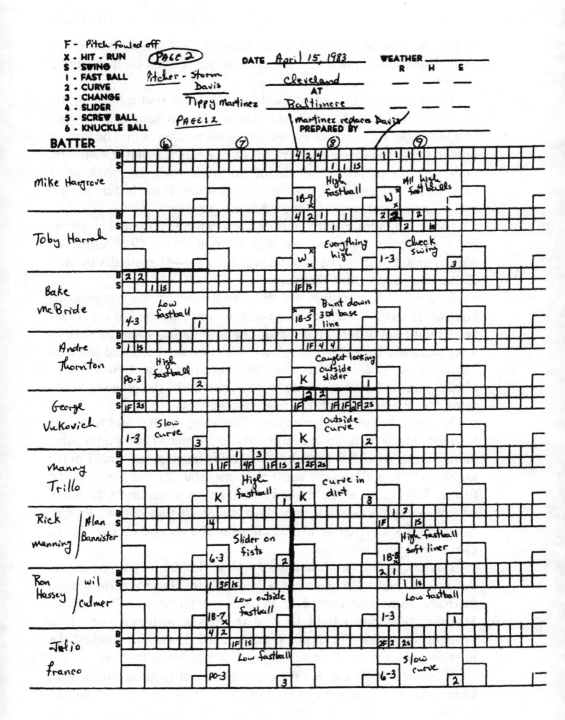

fastball he swung at. The result is marked "F-7," a fly ball to left field. The notes explain that it was a Palmer fastball on the outside corner.

This game was played on a cold afternoon in Baltimore. On the chart is a note that the wind was fifteen miles an hour and blowing in. One of the reasons Jim Palmer is a great pitcher is that he knows how to make the elements work for him. Realizing that it would be very difficult to hit a ball out of the park with the brisk wind blowing in, Palmer stuck with his high fastball. If the hitters hit the ball in the air, odds were it would be caught.

Eleven of Palmer's fifteen outs came off the fastball. The pitching breakdown chart reveals that Palmer threw 69 pitches: 43 strikes and 26 balls. The fastball was his key—46 fastballs to only 23 curves, sliders, and changeups.

In the first five innings Palmer also demonstrated tremendous control. He didn't walk a hitter and only once did he have a three-ball count on a hitter. That was in the first inning when he was 3–1 on Bake McBride. He came back with two fastballs and induced McBride to hit a line drive to the shortstop. The Orioles have always stressed that walks are to be avoided like the plague, something that Palmer himself has always practiced.

In the sixth inning Storm Davis took over for Jim and followed his lead. Many have compared Davis to Palmer. The two pitchers have similar windups, and like Jim, Davis has a great arm. I don't know if Davis will become another Palmer, but the kid has a terrific future. Davis retired the first two men he faced on fastballs. Then he got George Vukovich on a slow curve. If you notice, Palmer had retired Vukovich on a slow curve in the second inning. These charts tell you a lot.

Davis was fine until the eighth inning. Suddenly, everything he threw was high. He gave up a base hit to Hargrove on a high fastball. He walked Toby Harrah on four high pitches. Then Bake McBride beat out a bunt to load the bases with no outs. That brought up Andre Thornton. Davis settled down and worked the outside corner with his slider and caught Thornton looking.

Vukovich then came to the plate. A left-handed hitter with some power, Vukovich can be dangerous if he gets a pitch he can handle. Lefty Tippy Martinez was brought into the game, and he fanned Vukovich on a curve—the same pitch that had given Vu-

PITCHING BREAKDOWN

Baltimore 2, Cleveland 0

Team: Baltimore 130 pitches: 88 strikes, 42 balls

Jim Palmer: 69 pitches: 43 strikes, 26 balls
                      46 fastballs: 28 strikes, 18 balls
                      17 curves: 11 strikes, 6 balls
                      3 sliders: 2 strikes, 1 ball
                      3 changeups: 2 strikes, 1 ball

Storm Davis: 40 pitches: 25 strikes, 15 balls
                      25 fastballs: 21 strikes, 4 balls
                      7 sliders: 2 strikes, 5 balls
                      2 changeups: 1 strike, 1 ball
                      6 curves: 1 strike, 5 balls

Tippy Martinez: 29 pitches: 18 strikes, 11 balls
                      15 fastballs: 8 strikes, 7 balls
                      14 curves: 10 strikes, 4 balls

kovich fits all day. Tippy then got Manny Trillo on three straight curves.

When the game is over, it's important to review the pitching chart. A glance at this game reveals that Hargrove batted five times and took the first pitch on each occasion. That doesn't mean the pitcher should lob the first pitch down the middle. But you can get ahead of Hargrove in the count with a decent first pitch in the strike zone.

Examining the pitching breakdown chart shows a couple of things. As stated before, Palmer stayed with his fastball for most of the game. But he also had a fine curve—eleven of seventeen were in the strike zone. The pitching chart also says that Palmer allowed only one hit on a curve—a hanger hit to left by Julio Franco in the fifth inning.

It's easy to see why Davis ran into a few problems. He got twenty-one of twenty-five fastballs over the plate, but he threw fifteen other pitches and only four of them were strikes.

The curve is the best pitch for Tippy Martinez, and it worked

DEFENSIVE POSITIONING FOR ANDRE THORNTON

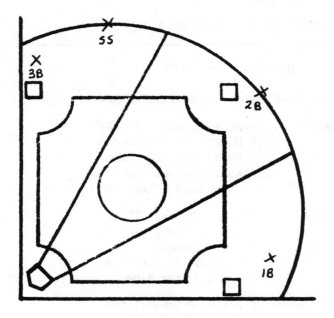

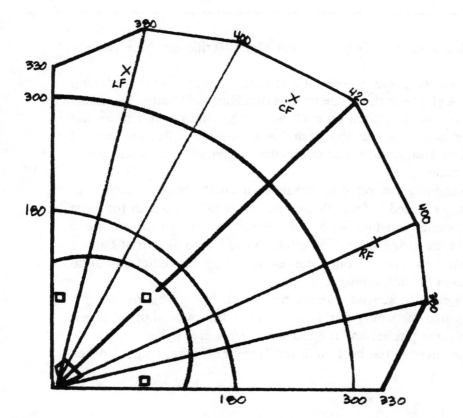

DEFENSIVE CHART

BATTER ANDRE THORNTON   BATS RIGHT THROWS RIGHT

JIM PALMER

OFFENSE

STRENGTH: POWER HITTER — SELDOM BUNTS OR STEALS A BASE

POWER ZONE: INSIDE FASTBALL; LOVES TO PULL ANY INSIDE PITCH

WEAKNESS: SLOW STUFF OUTSIDE; TRIES TO PULL THE PITCH AND TENDS TO POP IT UP OR HIT A GROUNDER TO THE SHORTSTOP

STRIKE OUT PITCH: SLOW CURVE

DEFENSE

OUTFIELD: GENERALLY DEEP AND TOWARD LEFT
RIGHT: STRAIGHT AWAY AND DEEP
CENTER: DEEP AND TO LEFT CENTER
LEFT: DEEP AND TOWARD 3RD BASE LINE
INFIELD: PLAY TO PULL
1ST BASE: NORMAL POSITION
2ND BASE: A FEW STEPS AWAY FROM BAG - DEEP AND TO PULL
3RD BASE: DEEP AND GUARD THIRD BASE LINE
SHORTSTOP: DEEP AND IN HOLE

DEFENSIVE POSITIONING FOR BUDDY BELL

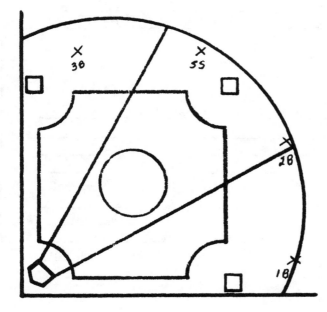

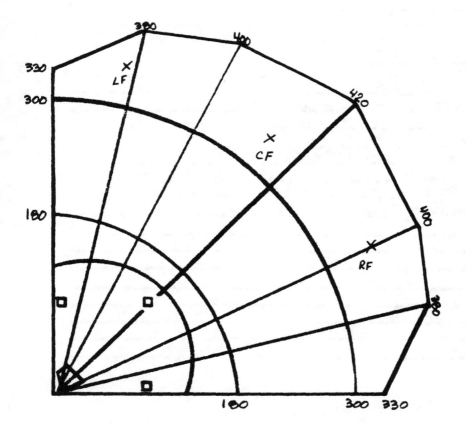

DEFENSIVE CHART

BATTER BUDDY BELL   BATS RIGHT THROWS RIGHT

PITCHER

JIM PALMER

OFFENSE

STRENGTH: Line drive hitter with some power. Seldom bunts — can steal a base — decent hit and run man.

POWER ZONE: Likes high fastball over the plate He will pull this pitch.

WEAKNESS: Fastballs inside and breaking pitches away

STRIKE OUT PITCH: Fastball on fists

DEFENSE

OUTFIELD: Somewhat deep and toward left field.
RIGHT: Play to pull and deep
CENTER: Somewhat deep and to left center
LEFT: Deep and toward line
INFIELD: Play straight away
1ST BASE: Shade toward line on breaking pitches.
2ND BASE: straight away
3RD BASE: Deep and toward line
SHORTSTOP: Deep and toward second base

Note: Bell will hit ground balls to all fields. When he hits the ball in the air, he tends to pull it.

well for him. He threw fourteen of them, and ten were in the strike zone.

Because the information derived from the pitching chart can help win a game, it is crucial that the person keeping it do a good job and pay close attention. Some teams use the next day's starting pitcher to handle the chore. That way the pitcher will keep a close watch on the hitters he'll be facing. On other clubs the chart is kept by a coach. So long as the chart is accurate, it doesn't matter who keeps it.

The Defensive Chart

The Orioles have charts on every hitter in the American League that show where they hit the ball against Baltimore pitchers.

Here are the charts for Andre Thornton and Buddy Bell against Jim Palmer. Thornton is a pull hitter no matter who is pitching. He likes the ball inside and prefers the hard stuff. For that reason we play him toward left field and deep. But Thornton will occasionally hit the ball to dead right field, and he has been doing this more in recent years. That's why the first baseman and the right fielder play him at normal depth. Bell is played more straightaway, because he hits to all fields.

Personally I never cared where Thornton hit the ball against Boston pitchers or anyone else—only against the guys who pitched for me. It didn't help me to know where Thornton hit the ball against Mickey Lolich; I wanted to know where he hit it against Jim Palmer and Mike Flanagan.

Another aspect to remember is that hitters and pitchers change over the years. As a young player Boog Powell seldom pulled the ball. But as he matured, he turned into a powerful pull hitter. For this reason you constantly have to update your charts.

THE PENNANT RACE

Scoreboard-Watching and
Lucky Pens

THE WORLD SERIES is the ultimate thrill. When a player signs his first pro contract, getting to the playoffs and the World Series is in the back of his mind.

Everything you do from the first day of spring training on is designed to get you to the Series. But to get there you've first got to win that pennant, more often than not in a race down the stretch. And that's why my teams always seemed to have an edge. Check the records: we almost always had a better record from September 1 to the end of the season than we had up to that point.

One of the reasons for my good September record is that by then I've settled on my players and have their roles well defined. I know who's doing the job in relief or as a pinch hitter and who isn't. No player's going to get that extra chance in September; either they've done it before now or they haven't, and if they haven't they won't be playing. In early July you might still be playing someone who's been having a difficult time, because you think that if you're going to win the pennant you'll need him. But in September you go with your best players for that particular year.

If there are only three starting pitchers doing the job, you might cut your rotation from the usual four or five down to three. I prefer a four-man rotation, but on occasion I have used three starters. You can get away with it in September, because there are more off days in the schedule, and that gives your pitchers extra rest. Under this system your fourth starter becomes a spot starter, pitching only when he's needed because the games have jammed up on the schedule. The man who was the fifth, or spot starter then becomes a long reliever, strengthening that part of your staff. You can't do this in the summer, during the heart of the baseball season, because the players will run out of steam. But in September you can, and it gives your best pitchers the most innings.

EARL WEAVER'S REGULAR-SEASON RECORD BEFORE AND AFTER SEPTEMBER 1

Year	Before Sept. 1		After Sept. 1	
1968	36–20	.643	12–14	.462
1969	91–43	.679	18–10	.643
1970	86–47	.647	22–7	.759
1971	81–48	.628	20–9	.690
1972	67–57	.540	13–17	.433
1973	76–54	.585	21–11	.656
1974	66–65	.504	25–6	.806
1975	73–60	.549	17–9	.654
1976	68–61	.527	20–13	.606
1977	75–55	.577	22–9	.710
1978	72–60	.545	18–11	.621
1979	87–45	.659	15–12	.556
1980	76–52	.594	24–10	.706
1981	42–32	.568	17–14	.548
1982	72–58	.554	22–10	.688
1985	37–33	.529	16–19	.457
1986	65–65	.500	8–24	.250
TOTALS	1,170–855	.578	310–205	.602

It also helps if you get some specialists from the minors when the rosters expand from twenty-five to forty players on September 1. I believe in using these extra players, even if it's only to pinch-run or for defense. If you don't think they can play, why promote them? You can use these players' best skills even if they only go in a game in certain special spots. They could be enough to give you that one extra game, and in a pennant race one more win can make all the difference.

In 1982 I used John Shelby in center during September instead of Al Bumbry. Bumbry had some leg troubles. Even though Shelby had spent the year at Rochester, he was a better defensive outfielder at the time than Bumbry. Also, Bumbry was playing hurt. I felt Shelby's arm and speed were better than Bumbry's, and I had to have the kid in the lineup.

Those extra players in September give the manager the freedom to make more moves. When you only have twenty-five players, you might hesitate to take a good defensive player out of the lineup for a pinch hitter. But if you have a kid from the minors who has a good glove sitting on the bench, then you go ahead and pinch-hit. You can also use extra pinch runners, knowing that your bench isn't going to run short.

In April, May, and June you don't know who your "Mr. September" will be. In July you still might be hoping for one guy to come back. But in September the players going well are out there every day, and any of them can become a Mr. September for you. I've seen players like Eddie Murray and Ken Singleton come back strong after a bad first half and really hit in the second half and in September in particular. Also, you've got all the statistics from that season, so you've got more up-to-date data to consider.

To win a pennant you have to have some guys get hot down the stretch. A guy who sizzles in September can make the whole season. From 1980 through 1982 Eddie Murray averaged almost one RBI per game in September.

I love a pennant race. On the bench we watch the scoreboard give a running account of the other games. We root for clubs to knock off the other contenders—you know, saying things like, "Come on, Cleveland, beat the Yankees." That's a big part of the fun of being in a pennant race. Some managers say they don't watch the scoreboard, that they think only about what their club is doing. But I always enjoyed watching the scoreboard and checking the newspapers the next day to see who would pitch against the teams you were fighting for the pennant. It gets your blood going when so many games can affect what happens to your club.

I don't believe it's any easier to go to the park during the

WHAT IT TAKES TO WIN THE TRIPLE CROWN

There's no higher compliment for a player than to say he could win a Triple Crown. There are only a handful of players—a Robin Yount, an Eddie Murray—who can combine power and average well enough to have a chance for one. But that alone isn't enough; it takes super-human concentration, and maybe a little selfishness, too.

Eddie Murray is like Reggie Jackson in that his individual statistics might be a little better if the game were always on the line when he batted, which is the attitude needed to win the Triple Crown. In the late innings with an important runner on second base, Reggie and Eddie become better hitters. There seems to be more effort involved. If the Orioles are winning 9–2, Eddie isn't the same hitter as when the score is 3–2.

With these players it's a matter of concentration. They're thinking of the team. They figure that if the score is 9–2 the game must be won. What does one more hit here mean? Better to save the energy for tomorrow when one hit might make a difference. There are 162 games, and if a guy plays them all, as Eddie does, he's bound to get tired, no matter how well conditioned he may be. From the team's perspective there's nothing wrong with approaching the game like Eddie Murray and Reggie Jackson. Save your energy for tomorrow. But your individual statistics suffer. Giving up on an at bat every five or six games is going to amount to a lot of extra outs by the end of the year.

In a game that is a blowout I suppose every player may sort of give up an at bat once in a while. No one can totally concentrate for all six hundred at bats, although Frank Robinson came as close to doing so as anyone who has ever played. It seemed as though he never let up for a moment, no matter what inning or what the score. Frank realized that a 9–2 lead in the seventh inning isn't always safe. Frank's concentration surpassed Eddie's, but Eddie is young enough that he may change. He's improving every year.

pennant race than at any other time. When you go to the park, you're going to work. Believe me, if you're on a four-game losing streak, it's drudgery to go to the park. Of course if you're winning four in a row, it's a lot easier. But you're still worried about falling into a cold spell, like Boston in 1978, when the Red Sox got out in front and then blew a sizable lead, losing eighteen out of twenty. Managing in one of those streaks is damn hard work. Watching the lead dwindle eats at you. It's torture.

When your team is losing, you should switch personnel on the field. If a guy has stopped doing the job, give him a rest. Check with your coaches and get their opinions. Maybe they've seen something that you haven't. The coaches might know something about a player who isn't 100 percent healthy; the player might be taking extra whirlpool baths, for example, and you might not have noticed. Or maybe a pitcher is hiding an arm injury. Go to your general manager and see what he thinks; he's been watching the games, too. Don't be afraid to ask knowledgeable people for their opinions. No one person sees or knows everything.

When a player is in a slump, it's wise to sit down with him and tell him to relax, to let his talent come out and not try to do too much. You get different reactions from different players. Some guys admit that the trouble is nerves. Others say they're hitting the ball well but had a dozen line drives caught that week. A few will ask you what they're doing wrong. For a manager the game is always on his mind during the season, but it weighs more heavily when his team is losing. You try to keep a very positive attitude in the clubhouse, the feeling that today we can turn this around.

I don't believe in momentum. You could be on a five-game winning streak and then run into Nolan Ryan, who will take care of your momentum by giving up no hits. After Ryan's no-hitter no one remembers that you had momentum. The thing about streaks is that they are so extreme. In a winning streak just about everyone is going well, or you wouldn't be winning. In a losing streak, just about everyone is going terrible. In those losing streaks, the anxiety factor is so paramount. Everyone wants to be the guy who stops it. The players try to take it all on themselves, but that just increases the pressure and makes the situation worse. A pitcher thinks that if he goes out and throws a shutout the streak is over. A hitter thinks that if he can hit three homers in a game, we'll probably win.

State of mind is so important. Take a pitcher who hasn't been backed by any runs in his last three starts. In the third inning, he gets a man on third with no outs. He's thinking that he can't let this guy score or else he'll lose. He tells himself to make the perfect pitch. He keeps aiming for the corners. Two batters later, the bases are loaded, thanks to walks. Then the next batter hits a double, and the pitcher is down 3–0 because he was worried about losing 1–0. Instead of throwing the ball over the plate and maybe allowing a sacrifice fly and one run, he's coughed up three runs. It's like Murphy's Law, and it doesn't end until someone pitches a great game or the offense breaks loose for a bunch of runs. You know the slump is going to end, but when you're in one it seems like it'll last forever.

SUPERSTITIONS

I'm not superstitious, although of course I know that a little bit of luck can go a long way toward winning a close game. Over the years I've picked up a few habits. If we were on a winning streak, I'd write out the lineup with the same pen. When the streak was snapped, the pen went into the garbage, and I broke out a new one.

The lineup card was also part of an Oriole ritual. My coaches and I had a system of carrying the lineup card to home plate. We'd take turns. As long as the team wins, the same man takes the lineup card to the umpire before the game. When we lost, it was the next man's turn. We did a lot of kidding about who could put together the longest streak.

I won't check the scoreboard clock during a game. I don't want to know how long my club has been in the field. It's just another habit. So is banging the bat. When the Orioles were in a jam, I'd tell one of my coaches, "Bang the bat three times on the dugout steps." The coach did, and if the Baltimore pitcher escaped, the same coach would bang the bat during the next tight spot.

The key is staying loose. We had some fun with this stuff, and it took the pressure off. I don't know if these things ever helped us, but they never hurt. Sure, they're kind of silly, but they can keep you loose.

You can never let up in a pennant race. When you have an eight-game lead, there is this terrible fear that you'll blow it. No one wants to be a part of a club that blew one of the biggest leads in baseball history. If you have an eight- or ten-game lead, you should push yourself to win every game as if you were one game behind. You must keep going that hard until the pennant is wrapped up, and that way you'll probably avoid that fatal losing streak. I know, because I've been on both ends. Many of my clubs have gotten healthy leads and kept them in September. But there was the 1979 World Series, in which we had a 3–1 lead and needed to win only one of the next three games. We couldn't do it, even though we tried like hell. The possibility of blowing a lead is there, and it has happened time and time again in baseball history. Everyone thinks about it.

Experience is also a big advantage. That's especially true in a pennant race and in the playoffs. A team that's been through the playoffs before should have an edge over a club that's in the playoffs for the first time. Another advantage is to have a pitcher with some playoff experience. That starter has more of an idea what to expect the day before the playoffs, when the media is looking for interviews, and the day of the game. If there is a tremendous difference in talent, it's another story. By that I mean that if one pitcher has playoff experience but has won only seven games this season, he probably shouldn't start over another pitcher who has won twenty games, even if the twenty-game winner is in his first playoffs.

But when it came time to select the man I wanted to pitch the first playoff game for the Orioles, I went with the man who had the experience. In 1979, when the Orioles faced California, I had the choice of starting Mike Flanagan, who had gone 23–9, or Jim Palmer, who was 10–6. I gave Palmer the ball, because he was 4–0 with a 1.96 ERA in previous playoffs. Also, even though Jim missed a number of starts in 1979 because of injuries, he did awfully well when he took the mound. Flanagan had never been in the playoffs.

Each player will have different things to say about being in the playoffs, especially their first playoffs. But I'm still looking for that guy who can honestly say the playoffs didn't make him nervous. Some guys are surprised by the pressure in the best-of-five championship series. Obviously, some handle it better than others. But I firmly believe that experience is vital, because then the playoffs are not uncharted territory.

I managed in six playoffs, and each time I was nervous as hell.

Everything you do is magnified. Every move goes under the micro-scope, and it really hurts if you lose. To make the playoffs, a team had to have a terrific regular season. For 162 games they were the best in their division. But three bad days in the playoffs, and your whole season goes down the drain. People may remember who lost in the World Series, but few recall what team was beaten in the playoffs. When a whole season's work goes on the line in a best-of-five playoff, it's enough to make the nerves swing into action. And then there's the matter of the paycheck. "To the winner goes the spoils" is the old saying, and it sure applies here. Sometimes the winner's share in the playoffs is twice as much as the loser's when you add that World Series money. With the big salaries, people may not think this is a factor. But players are like everyone else; they want to make as much as they can.

I don't manage differently in the playoffs than I do during the regular season. I make out the batting order the same way, and I start off the game watching: Does my pitcher have it? How are my hitters swinging at their pitcher? I don't do anything tricky in the early innings. I pay extremely close attention to my pitcher. If he's getting hit, I'll have to play for the big inning, hope to get a couple of homers. If both pitchers look good and one run will mean a lot, I might bunt or steal a base in the fourth, fifth, or sixth to try and get on the scoreboard. I play the late innings the same way as always.

In the playoffs there are so many writers around before the game that you have to walk around to get a view of the field. During the regular season you can get a good view from the dug-out. There are other little things a manager notices. He wants everyone on the field when they're supposed to be and no one sleeping in the dressing room. In the playoffs that isn't a problem.

No matter if it's a spring-training game or the playoffs, I watch batting practice. I won't see anything that will help me once the actual game begins, but a manager should make sure the players are getting their work in. The coaches hit ground balls and throw batting practice, but I like to make sure that the players get their swings and take their ground balls and that no one gets hurt.

Often, players who have produced in the playoffs before do well again. But the reason for that is that they had the talent in the first place. God-given ability is always the starting point. Also, the people in your lineup for the playoffs are almost always coming off good years; if they weren't, you wouldn't be there in the first place. A team in the playoffs is bound to have three successful starting pitchers: one guy isn't going to pitch you to a division title.

The bottom line is that over the long haul the best team usually wins. In a short series anything can happen, but on the whole my teams did all right for themselves down the stretch.

11

ONE CRUCIAL GAME

The View from the
Dugout

BEFORE the 1979 playoffs we knew the California Angels were a damn good team. We had won nine of twelve games against them that season, but that didn't give us a lock on the playoffs. As I said, all it takes are three bad days and you're sitting at home, watching the World Series on television.

California was a team that didn't have a lot of guys with playoff experience. But we were in the same boat. In 1979 the Orioles who had been through the playoffs were Jim Palmer, Mark Belanger, Terry Crowley, Al Bumbry, and Lee May. This was the first time the Angels had ever made the playoffs, but a few of their players had playoff experience with other clubs: Don Baylor, Bobby Grich, Merv Rettenmund, Bert Campaneris, and Joe Rudi. Ironically, Grich, Baylor, and Rettenmund had gotten their playoff experience with us. Another irony I learned was that the first game in the history of the California Angels franchise was played at Baltimore Memorial Stadium, just as their first playoff game was.

Before games like this I'd say a few words to the club. I told the players not to hurry, to make sure they did things the same way they had done them during the regular season, and not to try to be supermen and do things they weren't capable of just because it was the playoffs. It wasn't rah-rah stuff to try to psyche them up. In fact, it was just the opposite. You're trying to sort of tranquilize the team, to keep everything calm.

The Angels decided to go with Nolan Ryan. For his career Ryan was 5–13 against Baltimore with a 3.86 ERA. But Nolan Ryan is Nolan Ryan. He throws as hard as anyone. The man owns five no-hitters, and he can throw one at you any time he takes the mound. If you don't get a hit, odds are you aren't going to win. So you'd better believe I was concerned when we went up against Ryan. I knew we wouldn't get a lot of runs.

I took out my stats on how the Oriole hitters had fared against Ryan and made out my lineup. Here's how it looked:

1. *Al Bumbry, center field.* He had a nice season in 1979, hitting .285 with 37 stolen bases. He was a good leadoff man that season and hit around .250 against Nolan. There was no reason for me to change the leadoff spot. It would be idiotic to change at this point, anyway.

2. *Mark Belanger, shortstop.* Usually Mark was our ninth hitter. His lifetime batting average was in the .220s, but he was the best hitter I had against Ryan. Mark hit over .350 against Ryan's fastball. Mark had a short stroke and did very well against fastball pitchers. He was also seven for thirteen against Jim Kern and a .300 hitter off Goose Gossage. Mark's history against Ryan was the reason I moved him up in the lineup. Mark also had a good eye and could draw a walk. Ryan's control can be shaky, and if you give him a chance he might beat himself with walks.

3. *Ken Singleton, right field.* He batted third all year for us and had an outstanding season, so I had no plans to take him out of the third spot. The man hit .295 with 35 homers and 11 RBIs. He also drew 109 walks. He was patient at the plate, and that's important against Ryan.

4. *Eddie Murray, first base.* Eddie batted fourth all year and hit 25 homers and drove in 99 runs. Even though his stats were nothing special against Ryan, he stayed in the fourth spot.

5. *Pat Kelly, left field.* A good fastball hitter. In 1979 he hit .288 with nine homers in 153 at bats. Pat also had the ability to steal

a base, and a team can run on Nolan Ryan. That was another reason Belanger was high in the lineup. Mark has speed, and we had beaten Nolan by stealing off him during his career: he has a very slow move to first. A final reason Kelly was in left rather than Benny Ayala or Gary Roenicke was that I liked to have a left-handed bat in the lineup against Nolan. Roenicke and Ayala are right-handed hitters.

6. *Lee May, designated hitter.* Lee's numbers against Ryan were not very good, but he did have the ability to hit the long ball. In 1979 May hit 19 homers and was a .321 hitter against California. I often batted Lee fifth, but I dropped him to sixth because Kelly hit close to .300 off Ryan. Also, Lee didn't run very well. If Pat got on first and Lee hit a ground ball, Pat might get to the second baseman quickly enough to break up a possible double play.

7. *Doug DeCinces, third base.* Doug played third all year and like Kelly was a good fastball hitter.

8. *Rich Dauer, second base.* Dauer is one of the best second basemen in baseball. In 1978 he went 86 games without an error. With defense like that at second I wasn't going to worry about his bat.

9. *Rick Dempsey, catcher.* Rick was in there strictly for his defense. He threw out over half the runners who tried to steal against him in 1979, and I believe he has one of the best arms in the majors. He had trouble against Ryan, but my other catcher, Dave Skaggs, didn't hit Ryan, either. Skaggs's defense was not equal to Dempsey's.

Jim Palmer, pitcher. Jim wanted me to start Mike Flanagan in the first game. Flanagan had that great season, with 23 wins, and eventually was voted the Cy Young Award. Jim believed that if he pitched the first game of the playoffs, his arm wouldn't bounce back enough for him to pitch the fifth game. Jim was entitled to his opinion, but the manager selects the starting pitcher. I wasn't worried about the fifth game; if Jim won the first game, there might not be a fifth. Besides, if Jim couldn't pitch the fifth game, I had Steve Stone, who was 6–2 with a lifetime ERA of 3.36 against the Angels. Also, Jim was 21–8 for his career against California and 2–0 against them in 1979 with a 1.25 ERA. Finally, Jim had experience working for him.

Another consideration was the California lineup. The Angels had six regulars who were right-handed hitters. All of their power came from the right side: Don Baylor, Dan Ford, Bobby Grich, Carney Lansford, and Brian Downing. The three left-handed hitters were Rick Miller, Larry Harlow, and Rod Carew. I felt that Palmer's being right-handed would help him. (Flanagan is a lefty.) In almost every area you possibly could consider, Palmer seemed like the man to open the playoffs. He had the experience, and he had done well against California and their hitters during his career and during that particular season. Jim knows how to rise to the occasion. None of this should be taken as a slight on Flanagan, who is a fine pitcher in his own right. But Jim Palmer will be in the Hall of Fame, and it's hard to go wrong when you pitch a Hall of Famer.

Here's how the game went.

First Inning *California*—Rick Miller grounded out, and Carney Lansford struck out. Then Palmer got a fastball over the plate to Dan Ford, who ripped it over the left-center-field fence. (I always liked Ford and was happy when the Orioles obtained him before the 1982 season, even though he didn't play as well as expected; I wasn't at all surprised when he came back strong in 1983.) Don Baylor flied out to end the inning, but California had a 1–0 lead.

Baltimore—Al Bumbry, Mark Belanger, and Ken Singleton struck out. The radar gun had Ryan throwing around 94 miles an hour. This was his first inning in postseason play, but it's impossible to do any better than he did.

Second Inning *California*—Rod Carew grounded out to Dauer, Brian Downing grounded out to DeCinces, and Bobby Grich popped to Dauer. Palmer had settled down and was hitting his spots.

Baltimore—Eddie Murray struck out. Pat Kelly grounded out to Grich at second. I was glad to see someone finally hit a fair ball off Ryan. But he came back and fanned Lee May to end the inning. At this point, I was convinced it was going to be a pitcher's battle.

Palmer had good stuff, and Ryan—well, what can you say about a
guy who blows away five of the first six hitters he faces? Ryan was
throwing strikes, and I was wondering how we could get to him.
When Ryan gets everything over the plate, he's overwhelming. As
I said before, the man owns five lifetime no-hitters, more than
anyone in baseball history.

Third Inning *California*—Larry Harlow grounded out to
Murray. Jim Anderson, who gave us a tough time all year, hitting
.319 against us, grounded out to Belanger. Rick Miller, who has
good speed, hit a high chop to short and beat Belanger's throw for
a single. Miller then took second on a passed ball: Rick Dempsey
had problems with a Palmer curve. Maybe the fact that Dempsey
was in his first playoff had something to do with it; Dempsey had
caught 124 games for us and had only five passed balls all season.
Palmer then walked Lansford, putting runners on first and second
with two outs. Then Ford, who had only two RBIs against us
during the regular season, doubled in Miller for his second RBI in
three innings. Baylor grounded out to end the inning. California
had taken a 2–0 lead, but I thought Palmer was throwing well. The
only balls hit hard off him were by Ford. Miller's infield hit, which
was nobody's fault, had started the rally. In fact, if Miller had hit
the ball decently, it would have gotten to Belanger faster and he
would have thrown Miller out at first to end the inning. I was happy
with Jim, but not thrilled about being down 2–0 to Nolan Ryan.
Things weren't going very well. We had to get Jim some runs.

Baltimore—Doug DeCinces led off by hitting a fly ball into
short right field. Grich appeared to catch it, but it went off his
glove for a two-base error. When you consider that Grich has won
five Gold Gloves, you know we got a break there. It was one of
those things, like Dempsey's passed ball, that you don't figure will
happen. I was happy to have a runner on second with no outs.
Lord knows, we had to get something going soon. Rich Dauer was
the hitter. I've made it clear that I don't believe in bunting a runner
from second to third. Besides, we were down by two runs—but I
wouldn't have done it no matter what the score was. Also, Dauer
has the ability to hit the ball to the right side of the infield as well
as anyone on the club. A grounder to the right side would have
moved DeCinces to third and might even have scored him if it
went through the infield for a hit. So there was every reason to let

Dauer swing away. I did, and he hit a fly ball to left field for the first out.

When I put Dempsey into the lineup, I was thinking about his defense, but he came through with a run-scoring double. That made the score 2–1. Bumbry fanned for the second out of the inning. That brought up Belanger. Remember, he was a .350 hitter off Ryan. Mark came through with a run-scoring single to tie the game. When I put him up high in the lineup, I had no way of knowing he'd come through with a hit like that. I only hoped he would, and I had some information that said he could hit Ryan. This time it worked. Ken Singleton then walked, but Murray fanned to end the inning. The score was 2–2, and we were pulling for Palmer to hold them.

Fourth Inning *California*—Rod Carew led off with a bunt single. When Carew is up at the plate, the defense is aware of the bunt. But the man is one of the best bunters ever to play the game, and sometimes there isn't a thing to be done when the bunt is perfect. Downing grounded out, sending Carew to second. Grich walked. Palmer didn't want to give Grich anything good to hit with the eighth and ninth hitters up next. Nevertheless, there were now runners on first and second with one out, and the Angels were a base hit away from a 3–2 lead. But Palmer got Harlow on strikes, and Anderson popped out to DeCinces.

Baltimore—Kelly led off with a walk. The score still was 2–2. I never gave a thought to bunting, not with Lee May up. Besides, one of the reasons I played Kelly was that he could steal me a base. This was the ideal time to do it. With his slow delivery to the plate, Ryan gives the baserunner the advantage, and Kelly easily beat the throw to second. That put a runner on second with no outs. I repeat, I don't consider this a bunt situation, although someone else might. I let May swing, and he struck out. DeCinces was the next hitter. Ryan unleashed a wild pitch, sending Kelly to third with one out. DeCinces is a good fastball hitter, one of the better high-fastball hitters in the league, and I was confident he could make contact against Ryan, even though Nolan has enough ability to strike out anyone, anytime. I've stated that the squeeze play is the most dangerous play in baseball, and the fourth inning usually is much too early to go for it. Frankly, I never considered anything but letting DeCinces swing away. Doug did and hit a sacrifice fly to score Kelly. Dauer grounded out, but we had a 3–2 lead. Kelly was the key in this rally: he patiently drew the walk and stole the base, and then we made the most of the wild pitch.

Fifth Inning *California*—Miller flied out. Lansford flied out. Ford grounded out. In this inning Palmer did exactly what he should. He had a 3–2 lead, and he went out to the mound and got the ball over the plate, letting his defense work behind him.

Baltimore—Dempsey flied out, Bumbry grounded out, and Belanger flied out. Even through Ryan had given up three runs, only one had been earned and he was throwing very well. I knew that each run would be important. Just as in the early innings, I was thinking about getting runs one run at a time. It's not what I do every day, but you don't face a Ryan every day.

Sixth Inning *California*—Baylor popped out to Dauer. Carew singled to right. The man is a magician with the bat; no wonder he hits .300 every year. Downing fouled to DeCinces for the second out of the inning. That brought Grich to the plate, and he's always dangerous. The thing about Grich is that he is more than a Gold Glove second baseman and a .280 hitter. The man has power, and when you get that from a second baseman, it's a real plus. Grich doubled in Carew to tie the score at 3–3. That brought Harlow to the plate. I was a little concerned about Palmer, but he had struck out and popped up Harlow the first two times. Jim is also a very tough customer with runners in scoring position. He bore down and struck out Harlow again to end the inning. But the game was tied, 3–3.

Baltimore—Well, it was a tie game and once again the main concern was to get another run. Ryan got Singleton to hit a fly ball for the first out. Then Murray walked. That brought up Kelly. With one out it would be stupid to use the sacrifice bunt. Also, I had Kelly in the lineup because Pat had the second highest batting average on the club against Ryan even though it was under .300. Kelly came through with a base hit, sending Murray to second. May was the hitter. He drove in some big runs during his career, but this time he grounded into a double play, Grich to Carew, and the game stayed at 3–3.

Seventh Inning *California*—Jim Palmer was still throwing like Jim Palmer so I had no reason to take him out. Besides, Jim will let me know if he believes there's a reason to go to the bullpen. As long as he felt fine and was throwing well, I was sticking with him. Palmer had an easy inning, getting Anderson to pop out to Dempsey, Miller to fly out to Kelly, and Lansford to ground out, pitcher to first.

Baltimore—How could we get another run? That was running through my mind again and again. The way Jim was throwing, one more run might do it. But Ryan still had his stuff. He wasn't striking out people like he had done earlier, but that didn't mean he was any bargain. DeCinces grounded out. Then Dauer singled. I suppose I could have pinch-hit for Dempsey, but Rick had hit the ball well in the third when he had that RBI single. Besides, it still was a 3–3 game, and I needed Rick's arm. Rick slapped a looper into center field, and we all thought it was going to drop for a hit, especially Dauer, who was running from the moment the ball touched the bat. But Miller made a great running catch and easily doubled Dauer off first for an inning-ending double play. When something like that happens, you might think you won't get another run. But good teams shake it off, just in the way good teams make plays like Miller's.

Eighth Inning *California*—Ford was the leadoff hitter, and he flied out. That was a big out, considering how badly he'd hurt us in his first two trips to the plate. Baylor was the next hitter. Like Ford, he had the ability to win the game with one swing. Baylor batted only .196 against the Orioles during the regular season, but he had three homers. But I love having Jim Palmer on the mound. He is a master. Between his talent and his experience, he was giving us a great game in the playoff opener. I just hoped he'd continue to be careful. Jim did, as he got Baylor to ground out for the second out of the inning. That brought up Carew, who already had two hits. Carew did it again, with a base hit up the middle. Jim Fregosi was managing the Angels, and I thought he might want to get Carew to second base, where he could score on a single. Hell, I'd want that if I were in his place. The batter was Brian Downing. Carew has decent speed and can steal a base if the opportunity is right. He broke for second, but Dempsey gunned him down. It was a big play: if Carew gets to second, maybe Downing gets a hit to drive in the run. But we'll never know, because Downing didn't get that chance, thanks to Dempsey's defense.

Baltimore—We had been in close games all season. In fact 86 of our 159 regular-season games were decided by two runs or less. We had more close ones than any other club in 1979. We went 52–30 in those games and were 32–20 in one-run games. Both of those were the best marks in the American League. One last thing: in games tied from the seventh inning on, we were 36–23. At the time I didn't know all of these exact statistics, but I did know we had been in a hell of a lot of close ones and had won our share. I was pulling for us to do it again. As had been the case all night, I was thinking about how we could get another run. But in this inning Ryan didn't come out to pitch. They said he had pulled a groin muscle. How fortunate. That isn't to say anything bad about the reliever, John Montague, but Ryan is an awesome pitcher. He struck out eight in the first four innings and gave up only four hits. Montague had been in the Orioles farm system, although he had never pitched in the big leagues for us. He had started the year with Seattle and had been traded. He was mostly a breaking-ball pitcher, which made him a big change from Ryan. Also, he didn't throw nearly as hard as Nolan. Few pitchers do. But we didn't do much in the bottom of the eighth: Bumbry flied out, Belanger grounded out, and Singleton popped out. The score remained 3–3.

Ninth Inning *California*—Palmer continued to do the job. He got Downing to ground out to Belanger, Grich to fly out to Singleton, and Harlow to ground out to Belanger. Jim was excellent. He had kept us in the game, and now we needed one more run to win it.

Baltimore—Montague was still pitching for the Angels. During the regular season we hit him pretty well. In 1979 Montague pitched against us five times and had an 11.68 ERA. In twelve and a third innings we got to him for sixteen runs. His career ERA against Baltimore was 8.53. Sometimes that means you own a guy. But stats have a way of turning around on you. Just because you hit a guy in the past doesn't mean you will definitely do it again in the future. Later, I found out that Jim Fregosi said Montague had won the division title for his club. In his first ten days with California he made seven appearances, picking up two wins and saving the other five games. So in the second half of 1979 Montague was pitching as well as he ever had.

Eddie Murray led off the bottom of the ninth for us by drawing a walk. Eddie doesn't steal many bases during the regular season, but he can run. Also Eddie only goes when a stolen base will mean something—in the late innings of a close game. Frank Robinson did the same thing. I gave Eddie the sign to go if he had the jump. He was trying to get a lead, but he strayed too far from first and Montague picked him off. What was happening at this juncture was that both clubs were getting anxious. Hitters were swinging at pitches they probably would have taken during the regular season, maybe even earlier in the game. Each guy wanted desperately to get the hit that would start the winning rally. Hitters were ahead in the count 2–0, but they would swing at a pitch in the dirt because they were anxious, and ground out. I've seen it happen over and over in the playoffs, the World Series, and crucial regular-season games. We remind our players to relax and be patient, but those things are easier said than done. Some players try to do things they can't. You'll see singles hitters trying to hit the ball over the wall. They'll go after a low outside pitch they normally would take and try to pull it. So Eddie might have been a little too anxious to steal second. Kelly then fanned, and Lee May flied out to end the inning. It was 3–3 after nine.

Tenth Inning *California*—Jim Palmer had given us nine good innings. He gave up seven hits and three runs. He finished strong, allowing only one single in the last three innings, retiring ten of the last eleven men he faced. Jim isn't a guy who's afraid to say when he's tired. If he hadn't said the word, I would have let him start the tenth. But Palmer knows how long he can pitch, and I respect his opinion. Jim did as well for nine innings as I could have hoped, and it was too bad we couldn't get that fourth run for him so he could get credit for the win. Don Stanhouse was waved in from the bullpen. Stanhouse was great in 1979, getting 21 of our 30 saves. He was also 7–3 with a 2.84 ERA. In this situation a manager is going to bring in his best relief pitcher, and for us that was Stanhouse. Fregosi had Willie Davis, whom the Angels picked up from the Mexican League for the stretch drive. He was a sound veteran who had played in the World Series for the Dodgers. Davis hit for Jim Anderson and grounded out. Rick Miller grounded to Belanger for the second out, and Lansford hit a fly ball to Bumbry to end the top of the tenth. The fact that Stanhouse retired the side in order was another indication that the hitters were swinging at pitches they would usually take. During the regular season he walked 51 in 73 innings, which is a very high ratio for a relief pitcher. But Stanhouse never throws anything down the middle. Every pitch goes for the corner. That was his way, and it worked. But you could count Stanhouse's one-two-three innings over the course of the season on one hand. Usually someone would reach base. In fact, some called him "Scare and a Save" Stanhouse, because he often pitched himself into trouble and then out of it. I called him "Full-Pack," because he'd make me so nervous I'd go through a full pack of cigarettes by the time he got out of a jam. But this time Don did exactly what we wanted. I was still looking for that last run.

Baltimore—Montague was on the mound for his third inning of work. I was still reminding the guys to relax and get a good pitch to hit. DeCinces started us off with a base hit. Now there was something to work with. Dauer was the batter, and this was the time for the sacrifice bunt. One run was all we needed. Dauer is a pretty good bunter, so Rich had the bunt sign and he laid down a good one, getting DeCinces to second with one out. Dempsey was the next hitter. On the bench, I had Terry Crowley, John Lowenstein, and Benny Ayala. Ayala didn't have any stats against Montague and he was a right-handed hitter, so he was out. Crowley was oh for three against Montague and Lowenstein was two for three. First base was open, and I thought Fregosi would have Montague walk my pinch hitter. I went with Crowley, and they pitched to him. That surprised me some since the base was open, but it worked for the Angels, as Crowley hit a fly ball to center for the second out of the inning. That brought up Al Bumbry. I was hoping Al could get a single and end it for us. But he didn't get that chance. California didn't intentionally walk him, but they gave him nothing good to hit. That put Bumbry on first and DeCinces at second with two outs. By pitching around Bumbry, California forced Belanger out of the game and forced me to make a move. I'm obviously trying to win the game right here. I had my gun loaded with my pinch hitters waiting—Ayala and Lowenstein still on the bench. I went to Lowenstein. Montague got two quick strikes on John. Then he threw an off-speed pitch on the outside corner, and the left-handed-hitting Lowenstein lined it down the left-field line. I thought the ball would hit the wall, but it went inside the left-field foul pole for my favorite weapon—the three-run homer. I remember we were all so excited that we ran on the field as John made his way around the bases.

Beating Ryan in the opener was clearly a big lift to the Orioles. We went on to win the playoffs in four games. I refuse to say one game is the "key," because they are all important in the playoffs and World Series. In the 1979 World Series we were in front 3–1 in games. We also had Flanagan, Palmer, and McGregor to try and win that last one for us, but we couldn't do it. So if there is a "key" game, it's the one you win that ends the playoffs or Series. But winning the opener is a great way to start.

You can't say enough about the way Jim Palmer pitched in that playoff opener. Because he had been through it before, he wasn't afraid to make a decision on the mound. He threw what he wanted, where he wanted it. He took the responsibility to shake the catcher off. When you have a guy with talent and experience, go with him. The only way I would have bumped Palmer for someone else would have been if the Angels had beaten him seven straight times.

This first playoff game shows what can happen when things go right for a manager, but the manager is always at the mercy of his players. All a manager can do is put the best guys into the game and hope they come through. If they don't, he loses.

GAME OF WEDNESDAY, OCTOBER 3, AT BALTIMORE (N)

California	AB	R	H	RBI	PO	A	Baltimore	AB	R	H	RBI	PO	A
Miller, cf	5	1	1	0	2	1	Bumbry, cf	4	1	0	0	3	0
Lansford, 3b	4	0	0	0	0	3	Belanger, ss	4	0	1	1	0	5
Ford, rf	4	1	2	2	3	0	Lowenstein, ph	1	1	1	3	0	0
Baylor, dh	4	0	0	0	0	0	Singleton, rf	3	0	0	0	1	0
Carew, 1b	4	1	3	0	8	1	Murray, 1b	2	0	0	0	13	1
Downing, c	4	0	0	0	9	0	Kelly, lf	3	1	1	0	3	0
Grich, 2b	3	0	1	1	1	3	May, dh	4	0	0	0	0	0
Harlow, lf	4	0	0	0	4	0	DeCinces, 3b	3	2	1	1	2	3
Anderson, ss	3	0	0	0	1	2	Dauer, 2b	3	0	1	0	3	3
Davis, ph	1	0	0	0	0	0	Dempsey, c	3	1	1	1	4	1
Campaneris, ss	0	0	0	0	0	0	Crowley, ph	1	0	0	0	0	0
Ryan, p	0	0	0	0	0	0	Palmer, p	0	0	0	0	1	1
Montague, p	0	0	0	0	1	1	Stanhouse, p	0	0	0	0	0	6
TOTALS	36	3	7	3	29	11	TOTALS	31	6	6	6	30	14

```
California          1 0 1   0 0 1   0 0 0   0—3
Baltimore           0 0 2   1 0 0   0 0 0   3—6
```
Two out when winning run scored.

California	IP	H	R	ER	BB	SO	Baltimore	IP	H	R	ER	BB	SO
Ryan	7	4	3	1	3	8	Palmer	9	7	3	3	2	3
Montague (L)	2 2/3	2	3	3	2	1	Stanhouse (W)	1	0	0	0	0	0

Error—Grich. Double plays—California 2. Left on base—California 5, Baltimore 3. Two-base hits—Ford, Dempsey, Carew, Grich. Home runs—Ford, Lowenstein. Stolen base—Kelly. Caught stealing—Carew, Murray. Sacrifice hit —Dauer. Sacrifice fly—DeCinces. Wild pitch—Ryan. Passed ball—Dempsey. Umpires—Barnett, Ford, Evans, Denkinger, Clark, and Kosc. Time—3:10. Attendance—52,787.

HOW NOT TO GET FIRED

All It Takes Is a .583 Winning
Percentage

THEY SAY managers are hired to be fired, but I was never axed from a baseball job at any level.

You want to know how not to get fired? It's easy. Win. And keep winning. And then get along with the front office. Remember you work for the owner and the general manager. Oh, you have to tell them what's on your mind and what you believe should be done, but they are the bosses.

Some people say I'm a hard person to get along with. I don't buy it. I worked for two owners and three general managers when I managed the Orioles; I was and still am dedicated to the organization. That is why I reject the notion that I could not work for someone like George Steinbrenner. It's purely a hypothetical situation, but suppose I became manager of the New York Yankees under George. Well, I believe he and I could get along, because we both would have the same goal—winning. Also, I can deal with others' personalities.

I've always put the organization before my own ego. In 1956 I reluctantly became the player-manager of the Knoxville Smokies. My first move was to bench a second baseman named Earl

Weaver. I put in a kid named E. C. Welsh for me. It wasn't that Welsh was a much better player, but he was younger and maybe had an outside shot of making the majors. I knew by then that I wasn't going to make it as a player.

When I took over the Orioles in 1968, I told myself that every move I made was going to be right. Of course they all won't work out. But when I make a decision, I'm convinced it's the right thing to do and I take it from there.

I have never been without a baseball job since I signed my first pro contract at seventeen. For that I'm grateful. I have a good knowledge of the game, and I'm a good judge of baseball talent. I didn't lie to anybody, and I did my job to the best of my ability. I also put a ton of hours into my work. I was never afraid of doing a little extra, like going to Miami Stadium during the winter to make sure everything would be set for the start of spring training.

I don't know if other managers have the fear of getting fired in the back of their minds. I can't speak for them, but I never worried about getting fired. My overriding concern was how to win that particular game each time I went to the park.

Winning means everything. If a manager wins, the front office takes him back. It's that simple. Everyone wants to win or else they wouldn't be in the game. Unless a team wins, it doesn't make money. A winner means good things for everyone—the owner, the general manager, the manager, the players, and the fans. They all share in it. So if a manager keeps winning, he doesn't get fired. Oh, they can touch you if you're winning, but usually they won't. They can't really afford to.

After nine years in the minors, I was smart enough to realize I wasn't going to make the majors as a player. I saw people passing me up, and I knew where my career was headed. At twenty-seven I was still young enough to play in the minors, but I knew I wasn't good enough for the big leagues, which is the only place to play. I had left high school for pro baseball at seventeen. I had no experience in any other profession. I had been a hod carrier and had done other menial jobs in the off-season, but those weren't what I was looking for over the long run.

But when I became the player-manager at Knoxville for the last 34 games of the 1956 season I reached a point in my life where I had to make a decision. As a player I had no future; I had only limited experience in jobs away from baseball. Then in 1957 the Baltimore Orioles offered me a chance to manage their Class D farm club in Fitzgerald, Georgia, for $3,500 a year. I had been in baseball for nine years and felt I knew something about it: it was my field of expertise.

Until I was asked to manage the Knoxville Smokies, I had never thought about managing. I knew some scouts and minor-league managers, and I was aware that teams had jobs available in their minor-league organizations. I felt I could work in some capacity, even in the front office.

I had no idea where managing would lead when the Orioles gave me the opportunity in Fitzgerald, but I was happy that I could continue to earn my living in baseball. It enabled me to support my wife and family and helped pay the bills and put the kids through school.

I had ambitions to get to the big leagues as a player until I realized I didn't have the ability. But I didn't think about that as a manager. There were very few guys who made it through the minors and then became big-league managers.

It's impossible to say what qualities a manager needs. I spent thirty-five years in baseball—going from the Class D level, the bottom of the minors, all the way to the Orioles—and I needed every minute of it to know how to handle some situations. Generally you get better with more experience. You learn what to do when you pinch-hit for a player and he throws a bat; when to leave a pitcher in and when to take him out. It's all been valuable. A manager must learn what to do when he walks to the mound with the plan of removing a pitcher from the game and the pitcher says, "I ain't going nowhere. Get out of here, this is my game."

When I was suspended from managing the Orioles, Jim Palmer told George Bamberger, the pitching coach, that he wasn't coming out. In these situations a manager must be sharp. Bamberger just said, "That's fine, Jim. But you better get out of the way because Dick Hall is coming in to pitch, and I'm leaving." Jim left the field. He had no choice.

In baseball there are so many different situations.

When I took over the Orioles in July of 1968, we weren't scoring any runs. So after the All-Star game, I had a meeting to let the players know that some changes had to be made to get us some punch in the lineup. I told the players we were going to scramble for more runs, do things like bunting for base hits. I also eliminated the hit-and-run sign.

The scary part is not knowing how the players will react to your taking over as the new manager. I hadn't played or managed in the majors, but I had confidence in what I could do. I know I'm a good judge of baseball talent. I managed for ten years in the minors and learned a lot. I had an idea of what had to be done to get the Orioles going. I also knew that this was going to be like

EARL WEAVER'S MANAGERIAL RECORD

Year	Club	League	W	L	Pct.	Pos.
1956	Knoxville	South Atlantic	10	24	.294	8th
1957	Fitzgerald	Georgia-Florida	65	74	.468	4th
1958	Dublin	Georgia-Florida	72	56	.563	3rd
1959	Aberdeen	Northern	69	55	.556	2nd
1960	Fox Cities	Three-I	82	56	.594	1st
1961	Fox Cities	Three-I	67	62	.519	4th
1962	Elmira	Eastern	72	68	.514	2nd
1963	Elmira	Eastern	76	64	.543	2nd
1964	Elmira	Eastern	82	58	.586	1st
1965	Elmira	Eastern	83	55	.601	2nd
1966	Rochester	International	80	64	.565	1st
1967	Rochester	International	80	61	.567	2nd
1968	Baltimore	American	48	34	.585	2nd
1969	Baltimore	American	109	53	.673	1st
1970	Baltimore	American	108	54	.667	1st
1971	Baltimore	American	101	57	.639	1st
1972	Baltimore	American	80	74	.519	3rd
1973	Baltimore	American	97	65	.599	1st
1974	Baltimore	American	91	71	.562	1st
1975	Baltimore	American	90	69	.566	2nd
1976	Baltimore	American	88	74	.543	2nd
1977	Baltimore	American	97	64	.602	2nd (T)
1978	Baltimore	American	90	71	.559	4th
1979	Baltimore	American	102	57	.642	1st
1980	Baltimore	American	100	62	.617	2nd
1981	Baltimore	American	59	46	.562	2nd
1982	Baltimore	American	94	68	.580	2nd
1985	Baltimore	American	53	52	.505	4th
1986	Baltimore	American	73	89	.451	7th
MAJOR-LEAGUE TOTALS			1480	1060	.583	

those ten years in the minors. Sooner or later half the players were going to be calling me that little jerk, stupid, or whatever. That's inevitable. Players get upset at their managers the same way people get upset with their bosses. So I figured I might as well keep my head up and walk into that clubhouse the way I wanted to. Just be myself.

A manager does have to tell people bad things once in a while. They aren't happy when you pinch-hit for them or when you take them out of the game for a relief pitcher. They don't like it when you have to tell them that they're going back to the minors. The toughest part is when a minor-league manager has to tell a kid he's been released. You even get that on the major-league level. Believe me, it hurt to tell Lee May and Pat Kelly that we were not going to offer them contracts for 1980. These guys had done so much for me, and to let them know that they probably wouldn't be back with the Orioles . . . well . . . there was no easy or painless way to do it.

I understand that a general manager has one tough job. He not only has to get the best players he can, but he has to worry about his payroll. The general manager has a budget to live by. That payroll can kill you. If the team is losing money every year, the owner will come to the general manager and say, "Hey, what's going on here?" Decisions are made when you weigh who you must pay or lose. Sometimes you can't keep the players you like because of the budget. It's a fact of life. The general manager is in a difficult spot. Sometimes he has to pay a little extra to get the player he likes and hope to make up that player's salary with bigger crowds at the gate. It's a gamble. Sometimes a general manager will tell a manager that the team simply cannot afford a certain player. You can't do anything in those situations but figure out how to get by without that player.

Most managers go through periods when they'd like to have the power to make trades like a general manager. A manager watches the players, at least in his own league, all the time and thinks he might be able to get the right guy for the right price. Then the manager tells his general manager, but the general manager often has a different opinion. It can get discouraging. Some managers are able to make the final decisions on trades and on who comes up or goes down to the minors. Whitey Herzog does that in

St. Louis. But I don't believe a manager can handle things in the dugout *and* take care of all the general manager's duties, too. That's too much. A manager–general manager really would have one hell of a time negotiating the players' contracts. In fact, it might be impossible for the man who serves as the manager to handle the signing of players in the best manner.

To me, taking care of the contracts would be awful. I couldn't do it; I'd just give the players what they wanted. As a manager, I want the players happy on the field, so I'd give them all nice contracts. Given the choice, every manager will choose to have a player who's happy rather than one who isn't. But the general manager has to make the best deal he can for his owner. That also means not giving the players everything they ask for, thus making some of them unhappy. There was a time when Sammy Stewart came to me because he was bothered that he wasn't starting. He felt he had the ability to start and had done his apprenticeship in long relief. On most teams Sammy would have been a starter. The big money goes to the starters, and I'm sure that was in the back of his mind. But if the big money was there for a player no matter what he did, the player would accept whatever job the manager assigned him. It's a real tightrope act, trying to keep the players happy while balancing the books. I'm glad I never had to try it.

You win games one at a time. Win today's game, and then we'll think about tomorrow's. That's why the only streak I believe in is the one-game winning streak. You play games one at a time and win them one at a time. One of the greatest statements in the history of baseball is: "Play them one at a time." Even in a double-header, you have to play the first game first. If you can put seven of those one-game winning streaks together, then you really have something.

In my seventeen years of managing in the majors I made two giant mistakes, and they happened within seven days of each other in 1977. Both times I was looking too far ahead without staying aware of what was taking place at the moment.

A manager must think ahead. It's a necessity, a part of the job. A good manager has to do more than worry about this batter facing this pitcher. But the danger is in getting too far ahead. For this reason I try to keep everything written down in front of me. I have a lineup card posted with the reserves listed on the bottom. That makes it easy to keep track of who's batting, who's supposed to be on deck, and who's available to pinch-hit.

The first mistake came against Minnesota when I confused Larry Hisle and Dan Ford. We were losing 1–0, and the Twins had a runner on second. Ford was at the plate, with Hisle, the cleanup hitter, on deck. I simply was thinking that Hisle was batting instead of Ford, and I ordered an intentional walk. After the first two balls, I realized my error. I had my pitcher then go at Ford, but he walked him anyway. Here I had wanted to get around Hisle, and now he was at the plate with runners on first and second and no place to put him. I was really in a spot, because the guy warming up in the bullpen was for the left-handed hitter after Hisle. So I had my pitcher pitch to Hisle, and Larry drove in a run with a base hit. That made the score 2–0, and we eventually lost that game 3–2.

I suppose I couldn't wait to get Hisle up to the plate so I could walk him. I had the inning all figured out, but I made a simple mistake.

Against Chicago a week later the bases were loaded and the score was 4–4. Tony Chevez, who had recently been recalled from Rochester, was on the mound, and Scott McGregor was warming up in the bullpen. I was anxious to get McGregor in the game in place of Chevez. The batter hit a ground ball over the pitcher's right shoulder. Brooks Robinson ran over from third to cut it off, and I was already on my way out of the dugout waving in McGregor. I thought that Brooks had thrown the runner out at first and that there were runners on second and third. The next hitter was Jim Essian, a right-hander, and on the deck was left-handed-hitting Ralph Garr. I was going to have McGregor walk Essian to load the bases and pitch to Garr. I was saying that as I went to the mound, waiting for McGregor with Brooks. But Brooks said that I couldn't walk him. I looked around and saw the score was still tied and the bases were still loaded.

I couldn't walk Essian because Brooks had thrown the runner out at the plate and the bases remained loaded. Therefore, I had brought in the left-handed McGregor to pitch to the right-handed-hitting Essian, which is not the smartest baseball in the world.

MANAGERS WHO WERE FIRED OR WHO RETIRED DURING WEAVER'S ORIGINAL FIFTEEN-YEAR TENURE

NATIONAL LEAGUE

Atlanta Braves
1. Luman Harris
2. Eddie Mathews
3. Clyde King
4. Connie Ryan
5. Dave Bristol
6. Bobby Cox

Chicago Cubs
1. Leo Durocher
2. Whitey Lockman
3. Jim Marshall
4. Herman Franks
5. Joe Amalfitano
6. Preston Gomez
7. Joe Amalfitano

Cincinnati Reds
1. Dave Bristol
2. Sparky Anderson
3. John McNamara

Houston Astros
1. Grady Hatton
2. Harry Walker
3. Leo Durocher
4. Salty Parker
5. Preston Gomez
6. Bill Virdon

Los Angeles Dodgers
1. Walt Alston

Montreal Expos
1. Gene Mauch
2. Karl Kuehl
3. Charlie Fox
4. Dick Williams
5. Jim Fanning

New York Mets
1. Gil Hodges
2. Yogi Berra
3. Roy McMillan
4. Joe Frazier
5. Joe Torre

Philadelphia Phillies
1. Gene Mauch
2. George Myatt
3. Bob Skinner
4. Frank Lucchesi
5. Paul Owens
6. Danny Ozark
7. Dallas Green

Pittsburgh Pirates
1. Larry Shepard
2. Alex Grammas
3. Danny Murtaugh
4. Bill Virdon
5. Danny Murtaugh

St. Louis Cardinals
1. Red Schoendienst
2. Vern Rapp
3. Jack Krol
4. Ken Boyer
5. Jack Krol
6. Red Schoendienst

San Diego Padres
1. Preston Gomez
2. Don Zimmer
3. John McNamara
4. Bob Skinner
5. Alvin Dark
6. Roger Craig
7. Jerry Coleman
8. Frank Howard

San Francisco Giants
1. Herman Franks
2. Clyde King
3. Charlie Fox
4. Wes Westrum
5. Joe Altobelli
6. Dave Bristol

AMERICAN LEAGUE

Boston Red Sox
1. Dick Williams
2. Eddie Popowski
3. Eddie Kasko
4. Darrell Johnson
5. Don Zimmer
6. John Pesky

California Angels
1. Bill Rigney
2. Lefty Phillips
3. Del Rice
4. Bobby Winkles
5. Dick Williams
6. Norm Sherry
7. Dave Garcia
8. Jim Fregosi
9. Gene Mauch

Chicago White Sox
1. Eddie Stanky
2. Les Moss
3. Al Lopez
4. Don Gutteridge
5. Bill Adair
6. Chuck Tanner
7. Paul Richards
8. Bob Lemon
9. Larry Doby

Cleveland Indians
1. Alvin Dark
2. John Lipon
3. Ken Aspromonte
4. Frank Robinson
5. Jeff Torborg
6. Dave Garcia

Detroit Tigers
1. Mayo Smith
2. Billy Martin
3. Joe Schultz
4. Ralph Houk
5. Les Moss

Kansas City Royals
1. Joe Gordon
2. Charlie Metro
3. Bob Lemon
4. Jack McKeon
5. Whitey Herzog
6. Jim Frey

Milwaukee Brewers/ Seattle Pilots
1. Joe Schultz
2. Dave Bristol
3. Roy McMillan
4. Del Crandall
5. Harvey Kuenn
6. Alex Grammas
7. George Bamberger
8. Buck Rodgers

Minnesota Twins
1. Cal Ermer
2. Billy Martin
3. Bill Rigney
4. Frank Quilici
5. Gene Mauch
6. John Goryl

New York Yankees
1. Ralph Houk
2. Bill Virdon
3. Billy Martin
4. Dick Howser
5. Bob Lemon
6. Gene Michael
7. Bob Lemon
8. Billy Martin
9. Gene Michael
10. Clyde King

AMERICAN LEAGUE *(Cont.)*

Oakland A's	Seattle Mariners	Texas Rangers/Washington Senators
1. Bob Kennedy	1. Darrell Johnson	1. Jim Lemon
2. Hank Bauer	2. Maury Wills	2. Ted Williams
3. John McNamara		3. Del Wilber
4. Dick Williams		4. Whitey Herzog
5. Alvin Dark		5. Billy Martin
6. Chuck Tanner		6. Frank Lucchesi
7. Bobby Winkles		7. Eddie Stanky
8. Jack McKeon		8. Connie Ryan
9. Jim Marshall		9. Billy Hunter
10. Billy Martin		10. Pat Corrales
		11. Don Zimmer
		12. Darrell Johnson

Toronto Blue Jays
1. Roy Hartsfield
2. Bobby Mattick

Well, McGregor threw Essian a hell of a curve that was low and inside, but Essian ripped it down the third-base line, kicking up chalk and driving in three runs. That was the ball game.

For some reason I'll never know, I was thinking about everything but what had just happened on the field. My mind was on McGregor and Essian. Of course, McGregor did not have to give up the double, but that was one of those things. To this day I don't remember seeing Brooks make that play at the plate.

When two of these things happen so close together, you have to have a meeting with yourself to see what's going on. I also had a meeting with the ballclub. I told the players, "Look, we're not doing so good right now, and two of the games can be traced to something I did. I'm trying to do more than I'm capable of doing and I'm getting ahead of myself. I have to do one thing at a time like everyone else." Honesty is the best policy. Bring it out in the open. I wanted the players to know I wasn't giving up on them, and I didn't want them to give up on me. We're all human and make mistakes. The key is not to make too many.

In managing there are mistakes and mistakes. If I send Terry

Crowley in with the bases loaded to hit for Mark Belanger and Crowley strikes out, that's not a mistake. Or if I bring in Tippy Martinez to face Graig Nettles and Nettles homers, that's not a mistake. Those are moves that didn't work. There is nothing to apologize about. But these other incidents were mistakes.

Like everyone in baseball, a manager must concentrate and keep his head in the game every minute. It won't always turn out right, but you have to look ahead, try to get the right guy on the mound against the right hitter. You can't go one batter at a time, but you always must be aware of what's happening and of what might happen.

I don't worry about the manager in the other dugout, just his players. I've heard some managers say they liked to manage against certain people, but that isn't a concern of mine. Some managers will make more moves than others. Sparky Anderson, Gene Mauch, and Billy Martin aren't afraid to go to the bullpen, send up a pinch hitter, or try to make things happen in a game. The important thing isn't that the opposing manager is making a move, but what player is coming into the game. I don't react to the fact that Billy Martin is using a pinch hitter. Rather, I decide what to do based on the identity of that pinch hitter. It's very logical. There's no overt match of wits. When Martin managed the Tigers and had Gates Brown, the match of wits was that Martin liked to get Gates to the plate as a pinch hitter when he could win the game and I wanted to keep Gates on the bench. But the central figure in this was not Martin or me, it was Gates Brown.

Again, the only thing I concern myself with is knowing which managers would make a move and which wouldn't. Some guys just sit there and watch the game. That's their style, and I'm not saying it's right or wrong. Maybe they don't make a move because they don't have confidence in their bench. But any manager who had Gates Brown on the bench would get him into the game at the first opportunity. That's common sense.

Whether the Yankees' manager was Martin, Dick Howser, Bob Lemon, or Steinbrenner himself, he would go for a pinch hitter when needed because he had Oscar Gamble, Bobby Murcer, and Lou Piniella. Gamble and Murcer are left-handed hitters, and Piniella bats right-handed. Now, it was up to me to decide which of those guys I wanted up there. If I had a right-handed starter on the mound, I could bring in a lefty. Then the Yankees would probably counter with the right-handed Piniella. In this instance, I'd ask myself whether I wanted my right-handed starter to face Gamble or Murcer or my lefty reliever to face Piniella.

The game is not Earl Weaver versus Billy Martin. What can we do? Just make up our lineups. It comes down to the players. Oh, I would have my players swing away more than Martin. He would use the squeeze play more than me. Sometimes it works, and sometimes it doesn't. But all managers face the same decisions.

I don't believe a team's personality reflects that of the manager. That type of psychological trash is worthless. If a team is good, it knows it can win. If it's bad, it'll lose. What has given the Orioles and me confidence over the years has been our pitching. Whenever I went to the park, I thought the odds were in our favor because our starters were so damn good. If you looked at the latest line in the paper, the betting sheets, you knew the odds were in the Orioles' favor. That leads to confidence.

Some people say the Orioles have a fiery team or call me fiery. I don't know what that means. What's a fiery manager? One who argues with umpires? One who hollers at his players? One who gets into fights? When people say that about me, I think they're nuts. That's what I've thought all my life.

I argued with the umpires when I thought they made a mistake, and I hollered at my players when I thought they made a mistake. Other than those things, there isn't anything fiery or combative about the way I managed. With the Oakland A's, Martin's style may have been "fiery," what with all that running and squeezing. Me, I like to sit back and wait for the long ball. What could be calmer?

In the fifteen years I managed the Orioles I don't think my team had five fights with other teams. We didn't throw any beanballs and had almost no altercations. That doesn't sound fiery or combative or even feisty to me. I really can't say what effect a manager's personality has on a club. I always was myself and did and said what I felt was necessary.

All a manager can do is get his best team on the field for that game and see that the players know what their jobs are and how to do them. That's the whole point of all your work, from the drills in the spring to your last pregame meeting at the end of the year.

After that, it's all up to your players. You can do everything right and your players can do everything right and you're still not guaranteed anything. That's what's so great about baseball; you can never take anything for granted.

On the last day of the 1982 season, we played the Milwaukee Brewers in one game for the American League East title. We had our ace, Jim Palmer, going against Don Sutton, the Brewers' best pitcher down the stretch. We had just beaten the Brewers three straight times, and we were playing before our home crowd. Everything was right but the result.

Our book on Robin Yount said to pitch him inside. In the first inning Jim Palmer pitched Yount outside. Jim didn't feel he was throwing well enough to get the ball past Yount on the inside corner of the plate. So Jim Pitched him away, and Yount ripped it into the right-field seats. I reminded Jim that we were supposed to pitch Young inside. So later, Jim pitched him inside and this time the ball went into the left-field stands. His first two times up Yount hit homers, one off an inside pitch and one off an outside pitch, one to right field, and one to left. On days like that, there's just nothing you can do.

After that game was over and the pennant was lost, the fans in Baltimore gave me a long standing ovation. Ten, fifteen, twenty minutes after the game they kept on cheering, and I had to come out twice to acknowledge the cheers. It was a moment I'll never forget. I wish I could have given them one more pennant, but I don't have any regrets about anything I did in my years of managing. I did the best job I could, and we gave the fans seventeen years of outstanding baseball. No one in a Baltimore uniform ever gave less than 100 percent. You can't win every game, but you can give every one your best shot. And in the final analysis, that's all anyone can ask of a manager.

EPILOGUE 2002

The More Things Change,
The More They Stay The Same

A LOT HAS HAPPENED in the eighteen years since the original edition of *Weaver on Strategy* came out. While I enjoyed a brief retirement, the Orioles won the World Series with Joe Altobelli running the club, beating the Phillies in 1983. The Orioles brought me back in 1985 to try and squeeze some success out of a team very different from the Orioles teams I had been a part of. At that point, the Orioles were relying on older free agents, guys like Freddie Lynn and Lee Lacy. Lacy and Lynn were great players, but by the time we got them, they weren't the stars they had been before. We had a shot to win the American League East in 1986, but as we came down the stretch, we lost three starters and Freddie Lynn broke down, and our September was flat-out bad. That was also the year Eddie Murray's relationship with Baltimore changed. Eddie wanted to come back from a pulled hamstring and play but wasn't allowed to; meanwhile he was being unfairly accused in the papers of not trying to play hurt. After the disappointments of the 1986 season, and be-

This epilogue is the product of an interview with Earl Weaver by Chris Kahrl of the *Baseball Prospectus.*

cause I had enjoyed my brief retirement, it wasn't hard for me to decide to re-retire.

The timing was pretty interesting; right after I left, baseball had a great year for home runs in 1987. Later on, baseball in the 1990s would draw a lot of attention for all of the runs that were being scored. A lot of teams hit a lot of home runs, and Mark McGwire and Sammy Sosa and Barry Bonds would break and set new records. Some people have said it was as if the Earl Weaver brand of baseball was the only brand of baseball being played. With all of the home runs being hit, it was easy to forget that there are two parts to fielding an Earl Weaver offense, and that getting on base is the most important part. Strange but true, it seems that some general managers and managers still don't understand the value of the base on balls.

Considering the high-powered offenses of the last decade or so, and the complaints about so many runs being scored, it's worth going back over Weaver's Laws to see whether or not they still apply today.

Weaver's First Law

No one's going to give a damn in July if you lost a game in March.

This is still true, even with the amount of media coverage teams get in spring training nowadays. The most important thing a manager has to take care of in spring training still is picking his twenty-five players.

Weaver's Second Law

If you don't make any promises to your players, you won't have to break them.

Every year, you hear complaints about players who feel disappointed because they didn't get the job, role, or playing time they felt they were told they could expect. The easiest way to avoid this sort of thing is the same as it was when I managed: it's the manager's job to make decisions, not to create expectations about playing time that have nothing to do with performance.

Weaver's Third Law

The easiest way around the bases is with one swing of the bat.

I think we have this one pretty well covered. If there's one thing that players, managers, general managers, player agents, and fans really should understand in today's game, it's that this is still absolutely true.

Weaver's Fourth Law

Your most precious possessions on offense are your twenty-seven outs.

This is still the most basic aspect of the game, and still one of the most misunderstood. Not only do managers misunderstand it, players do too. A manager has to convince his hitters that they have to get on base for the next guy, and that no player can do it by himself. Sometimes that isn't easy. In the playoffs, you can get into trouble because everybody wants to be a hero.

Weaver's Fifth Law

If you play for one run, that's all you'll get.

Sometimes where you play makes all the difference. In the mid-70s, we moved in the fences at Memorial Stadium ten feet. Why? Well, it does help you build an offense that can crank out big innings. If I had managed in the Astrodome my entire career, maybe I would have done things differently, but in most of today's ballparks, there is usually no reason to spend your outs on one-run strategies like the hit-and-run or the sacrifice bunt.

Whenever I'm watching a game, I'm always amazed when the announcer tells us that if a hitter gets the pitcher to 2–0 or 2–1, it's a nice time for a hit-and-run. Why should the hitter give up the advantage he now has? That pitcher wouldn't be in that situation if he could throw where he wanted to. The one guy I ever let hit-and-run was Rich Dauer, and I would either let him put the play on himself, or I'd signal him for it. But he was the only one. Brooks Robinson would hit into a lot of double plays, and some managers might have asked him to hit-and-run to avoid them, but with his power, I always felt it was worth the risk.

Weaver's Sixth Law

Don't play for one run unless you know that run will win a ballgame.

There are a few times to get fancy on offense, such as the bottom of the eighth or ninth inning in a tie game, or the top of the ninth if you're on the road, but you had better be doing it with a player who can bunt or who can steal bases with a really good chance of success. Even then, you had better have the right combination of hitters on-deck or on your bench to drive home that runner you just spent or risked one of your outs to advance.

Weaver's Seventh Law

It's easier to find four good starters than five.

I firmly believe that the four-man rotation would still work, even in today's game. It goes back to how you break people into the game, from the lowest levels of the minors on up. If your organization controls how much you have a young starter throw, keeping him down around five or six innings pitched, and you have more minor league affiliates to make sure you were using all of your starting pitcher prospects regularly, it would work. It's going to take a lot of educating to remind people that during my era, a lot of pitchers in the American League, with the designated hitter, were starting every fourth day, and that those pitchers had long and productive careers.

However, I'm realistic. Nobody is about to bring back the four-man rotation. With multi-year contracts and free agency, there aren't a lot of veteran pitchers today who will try something different if they think it puts their livelihood at any risk. Complete games and innings pitched used to be critical to a pitcher's chances of making big money in the off-season, but that isn't the case now.

Weaver's Eighth Law

The best place for a rookie pitcher is long relief.

A good, or better yet, a great rotation makes this a lot easier to do. We've seen the Atlanta Braves do this for a few years now with some rookie relievers. It doesn't hurt to get a guy into the big leagues this way, you just need to make sure he gets real work, not just partial innings here and there using him as the last man on the staff.

Weaver's Ninth Law

The key step for an infielder is the first one—left or right—but *before* the ball is hit.

This is one of those truths that is timeless. You would have a hard time noticing a great defensive player like Paul Blair, Mark Belanger, or Brooks Robinson take their first steps, because they'd already taken them by the time you followed the ball off of the bat to where they were setting up to field it. Great defense is a product of years of hard work and conditioning. The Orioles always had an advantage because they had players who understood this and who took this part of their jobs seriously.

Weaver's Tenth Law

The job of arguing with the umpire belongs to the manager, because it won't hurt the team if he gets thrown out of the game.

The players are what's important to the team's shot at winning a game, and you should make sure your team has everybody at it's disposal to win that game, even if it means you, the manager, have to hit the showers early. But if Lou Piniella can go a year without getting thrown out, then it looks like the umpiring must be pretty good these days.

Overall, that doesn't seem too shabby. Weaver's Laws have held up pretty well. Individually, these ideas might not have been pioneering concepts; I owe a lot to George Kissell, and Paul Richards was responsible for getting me thinking about how to handle cutoffs and relays. But I also came up with a lot on my own, and that added up to the Weaver brand of baseball. Keeping cards on what my players and the opponent's players had done was new at the time, but I wasn't doing anything very different from what Casey Stengel or the other great managers in the old eight-team leagues could do for themselves in their heads. But after I started keeping track of this kind of thing, eventually managers like Tommy Lasorda and Tony LaRussa would call and start asking questions. I gained some fame for my willingness to platoon players, but that wasn't by design. Ideally, would I rather have Barry Bonds than a platoon in left field? Of course, but not everybody gets to have Barry Bonds, and if instead you build a platoon that lets the players in the platoon do what they do well, you can compete against the team that has the best hitter in the league.

A key element of running a ballclub was taking advantage of the personnel that was on the roster. How you fill your twenty-five roster spots is just as important during a season as your twenty-seven outs are in a single game. For that reason, a good manager is one who works well with his general manager. A general manager should be asking his manager "what do you think you need?" Then he can go out and try and get it for you, and together, you help each other build a better big league ballclub. Looking back, I think the only time I ever strongly disagreed with my general manager was when we lost Doug DeCinces to the Angels before 1982, but that was in part because I had this vision of having a left side of the infield of DeCinces and Cal Ripken Jr., hammering fifty home runs and making my job easier.

Together, the manager and the general manager need to be able to rely on their scouts and minor league personnel. You shouldn't shake these things up every two or three years, because you need to have confidence in the judgment of the people you're working with. Minor league managers can be major assets to their organization if they can do a few things well. A good minor league manager needs to be a good judge of talent, with the ability to accurately project how high each player on his team can go. He also needs to be able to evaluate his players on the level of whether or not they can help the big league club at a particular time, especially as a September call-up. Is the player ready to play defense in the majors, or can he run, or is he ready to pitch in certain situations?

I've had some legacies as a manager. It's been good to see some of the guys who played for me go on to become good major league managers. When this book first came out, the guys who had gone on to manage had previously been on my coaching staff, guys like Frank Robinson, Jim Frey, and George Bamberger. Ray Miller finally did get his shot to manage a team. Since then, some of my ex-players, like Davey Johnson, Johnny Oates, and Lou Piniella have turned into some of the best major league managers around. Rick Dempsey and Lenn Sakata have managed in the minors. To be fair, I don't think Lou Piniella really learned anything from me about managing when I was managing him in the minors down at Elmira.

If there's one thing that's troubling about the game today from my perspective, it's thinking back on my lesson that "Ten Pitchers Are Too Many." I made the point that an extra pitcher usually ends up rusting in the pen. In today's game, with the focus on platoon matchups as every manager tries to have his own stable of situational left-handed relievers like Jesse Orosco or Rick Honeycutt, you're carrying guys who don't contribute an awful lot over a full season for the space they take up on a twenty-five-man roster. With some teams carrying eleven, twelve, or thirteen pitchers, you're seeing a lot of the strategy of the game disappear, as teams cut back on having quality hitters on their benches. I usually tried to have a couple of left-handed bats on the team, but who could also do different things with a bat in their hands. John Lowenstein was a good high fastball hitter, Pat Kelly was also good for hitting people who could throw hard, while Terry Crowley could hammer off-speed stuff.

But if you're carrying twelve pitchers, you're crowding your roster with relievers to face hitters that most teams don't have the space to carry any more. That means that there aren't a lot of guys who make it necessary for these situational left-handers to be brought in. So what good does it do to carry a reliever who's just going to get brought in to face left-handed hitters like Ken Griffey, Jr. or Barry Bonds, heavy hitters who couldn't care if they're facing a left-handed or right-handed pitcher? I generally used relievers as I needed them, and while it feels like you can't get enough pitchers

when you're getting bombed, you should only use two or three relievers in a single inning if things are going badly.

Trying to get that platoon matchup can lead to overmanaging. I
know, because I was guilty of it now and again. I remember a game
in 1980, when George Brett was flirting with hitting .400, and we
were in Kansas City in a tie game in the bottom of the ninth. Scott
McGregor was on the mound, and there were two outs, but runners
on first and second. Brett was due up, and I looked it up, and Brett
owned McGregor. You tell yourself "I'm not going to let George
Brett beat me," so I had to make a change. I only had Tim Stoddard
warmed up, a right-hander. On deck for the Royals behind Brett
was Amos Otis, and Otis hadn't done much against Stoddard in his
career. So I pulled McGregor, and brought in Stoddard to pitch to
Brett, but not really. I had Stoddard intentionally walk Brett, load-
ing the bases. At the time, I was thinking that with the game on the
line, I'd rather take my chances with that match-up—Stoddard versus Otis—than either McGregor or Stoddard against Brett. So Otis
stepped in against Stoddard, watched ball one, strike one, strike
two, ball two, ball three, fouled an outside slider down the first base
line, did it again, and held up on ball four. Game over, and we lost.
I got my matchup, but great moves on paper still need execution by
the players to work out. The players are good at what they do, so
many more of my moves worked.

Another example was a match-up of Graig Nettles versus Tippy
Martinez. Nettles was 1-for-21 against Tippy, and that one hit was
a homerun. Looking at those numbers, I brought Tippy in to face
Nettles with a man on first, and Nettles put two runs on the board
with his second hit and second home run off of Tippy. It was a good
move, and the numbers were there to say so. Remembering exam-
ples like this takes me back to what I've always said, going back to
the first sign I hung up in the Orioles clubhouse when I started my
career as a big league manager: it's what you learn after you know
it all that counts.

CPSIA information can be obtained
at www.ICGtesting.com
Printed in the USA
LVHW05s0345040818
585675LV00002B/2/P

9 781574 884241